Chicago's Midway Airport
The First Seventy-Five Years

Christopher Lynch

First Edition

LAKE CLAREMONT PRESS
www.lakeclaremont.com
Chicago

Chicago's Midway Airport: The First Seventy-Five Years
by Christopher Lynch

Published January 2003 by:

4650 North Rockwell Street
Chicago, Illinois 60625
773/583-7800; 773/583-7877 (fax)
lcp@lakeclaremont.com
www.lakeclaremont.com

Publisher's Cataloging-in-Publication
(Provided by Quality Books, Inc.)

Lynch, Christopher, 1966-
    Chicago's Midway Airport : the first seventy-five
years / Christopher Lynch. — 1st ed.
    p. cm.
    Includes bibliographic references and index.
    LCCN: 2001099073
    ISBN: 1-893121-18-6

    1. Midway Airport—History. 2. Aeronautics—Illinois
—Chicago—History.   I. Title.

TL726.4.C45L96 2002   387.7'36'0977311
                                 QBI02-200087

**Printed in the United States of America by United Graphics,
an employee-owned company based in Mattoon, Illinois.**

06 05 04 03 02   10 9 8 7 6 5 4 3 2 1

To my wife Cindy,
who has given me strength, inspiration, and three little miracles:
Pierce Thomas, Angela Elena, and Katherine Zoe

✈ **Publisher's Credits**

Cover design by Timothy Kocher. Interior design and layout by Sharon Woodhouse and Karen Formanski. Editing by Bruce Clorfene and Sharon Woodhouse. Proofreading by Sharon Woodhouse, Karen Formanski, and Ken Woodhouse. Index by Karen Formanski. Cover photo of jet by Peter J. Schulz, city photographer (courtesy of the City of Chicago, Department of Aviation).

✈ **Note**

Contents

✈ Part III: Boom and Bust, 1945–1963

✈ Part IV: Cleared for Takeoff, 1964–2001

Acknowledgments

➤It would have been impossible for me to put together a book on Midway Airport without the generosity of many people:

When I first decided to record the stories of Midway, Dave Allen, a friend who kept a Cessna at the airport, lent his considerable talents to the project by aiding in recording the many interviews with his arsenal of audio equipment. His eyes on the dials allowed me to concentrate on the interviews.

I would like to thank those who agreed to be interviewed for this project. Charles Downey, a naval aviator in the Pacific in World War II and recipient of the Distinguished Flying Cross, shared his stories about his experiences with American Airlines during Midway's heyday and the resurgence the field had with the arrival of Midway Airlines.

Philip Felper, a pilot with so many flying hours he lost count, recounted for me life at the airport during the era of the DC-3, a ship he flew for American Airlines.

Thomas W. Goldthorpe's wonderful drawings for this book help illustrate the early years of aviation, a topic that Tom knows very well. When Goldthorpe described the Wright Brothers experiments at Kitty Hawk, he did so in such detail that I could imagine myself standing there watching history unfold.

Robert Hill, whose book on the Clearing District, *A Little Known Story of the Land Called Clearing*, was a treasure trove of information, has an infectious passion for Midway's history. I thank him for his enthusiasm and faith in this project.

It was my lucky day when I met Harold "Checkerboard" Lind, for not only is he the leading expert on Maywood's Checkerboard Field and its role as an airmail hub, but also an ace photographer. Harold shot several of the photos within these pages, and for that I am most grateful.

David Young's book *Fill the Heavens with Commerce*, an account of pioneering aviation in Chicago, was my bible for this project. I was flattered that Young not only agreed to be interviewed for this book, but also to write its introduction. Anyone inspired to learn more about Chicago's aviation history should consult Young's book.

Photographs of the airport's history are surprisingly hard to come by because most reside in pilots' basements or attics. In my constant quest for photos, I was aided by

Robert F. Zilinsky, a former president of the Midwest chapter of Cross & Cockade, the society of World War I Aero historians. Mr. Zilinsky was extremely gracious in opening his spectacular archive of photographs and sharing its contents with me.

I would also like to thank Spero J. Melonides, David E. Kent, Bill Aitken, and James O'Hara for their input and photographs.

My profound thanks to Robert F. Soraparu for sharing his magnificent collection of rare Midway photographs. Bob's photos have greatly shaped this book, and I appreciate his generosity and enthusiasm for this undertaking.

My family's large collection of photographs was made manageable through the efforts of James B. Sloan, who helped catalogue and preserve them, making my job of selecting photographs considerably easier. Thanks also to Dean Del Bene for his enthusiastic support and the photos of his splendid Stinson.

Mike Rotunno was a legendary photographer at Midway Airport, and my most grateful thanks to Judy Anneaux and her sister, Mimi Ferrara, for sharing photographs from their late father's remarkable collection.

Thanks to Ann Roosevelt who took the time to interpret photographs from Franklin Roosevelt's famous flight to Chicago in 1932, and special thanks to Anthony K. Jahn, archive specialist for Marshall Field's, for giving me access to the Cloud Room material.

I also wish to recognize Commissioner Thomas R. Walker and all the fine people at Chicago's Department of Aviation. First Deputy Commissioner John Harris was very helpful in granting me permission to use Department of Aviation photos. Special thanks to Judith Hamill for her support.

Many thanks as well to Cathy Bazzoni of the city's Graphic and Reproduction Center Photo Bureau, and the talented professionals who tolerated my frequent visits there.

I appreciate the efforts of Lyle Benedict, reference librarian at the Chicago Public Library's Municipal Reference Collection, for his amazing fact-checking abilities.

Willy Schmidt, a retired photographer for the City of Chicago, captured the 1980s on film during the exciting rise of Midway Airlines. And Peter J. Schulz's photographs of the airport are nothing short of phenomenal. Thanks also to Chris McGuire for helping me meet deadlines, to Ray Padvoiskis for his assistance, Chris Kozicki for his support, and to Andy Pierce for his editorial suggestions.

My gratitude to Joshua Koppel, who researched and compiled numerous drawings of Midway's evolving runway layout and shared his extensive postcard collection on Chicago history.

My appreciation also goes to my agent Kevin Mullins, who saw the value of this material and the research I had undertaken and encouraged me to press on.

The story of Midway Airport received a wider audience thanks to Mike Leiderman, series producer of WTTW's fantastic series, *Chicago Stories,* who enthusiastically allowed Midway's history to be translated to television. My thanks also to Lucy Kinsella, Leonard Aronson, and Tom Siegel for their encouragement. And my heartfelt gratitude to Kathleen Quinn, whose professionalism and meticulous research as producer on the program "Midway Airport: Crossroads of the World" was inspiring. Whenever I would present Kathleen with a newly uncovered historical gem from the airport's past, she would repeat the mantra-like slogan of Chicago's legendary City News Bureau, "If your mother tells you she loves you, check it out." Thank you Kathleen.

Much of the information I know about Midway I learned from the late Fred Farbin, who worked at Monarch Air Service for over forty years and who often shared with me wonderful tales about the glory days at the airport. I am also very much indebted to the late Mike Rezich, who was a walking encyclopedia of aviation history and whose conversations about the early days were always enlightening.

My appreciation to Sharon Woodhouse, publisher of Lake Claremont Press. I am honored that she selected my manuscript to be added to the excellent titles Lake Claremont publishes. My editor Bruce Clorfene tackled the challenges unique to an oral history by making the narrative flow, yet allowing the individual voices to rise off the page. And thanks to Karen Formanski, assistant publisher, who took any last minute changes I made to the manuscript with humor and grace.

My appreciation to Mike and Rita Crosse, as well as James Deir, for all of their support to me over the years on this ongoing project. And I am grateful to my brother Brendan and his wife Jennifer for giving me a scanner for Christmas 2000. Although I did not know it then, that scanner would get a real workout in preparing this book. Thanks too to my brother-in-law Chad Chimenti for loaning me his expensive camera. My brother Terry and sister Katie were likewise supportive of my venture.

My mother, Sheila O'Carroll Lynch, has a unique perspective on Midway's history, having spent her youth around airplanes as the daughter of a pilot. Most of her baby pictures inevitably have a wing of an aircraft in the background. I thank her for her patience, as she tolerated my constant stream of questions about her memories of that era. I am also indebted to my father, Matthew J. Lynch, for sharing his insights and expertise about corporate aviation. My parents' love and support was indispensable to me and helped me push on with this book.

And finally, I would like to remember my grandparents, the late Pierce and Rose O'Carroll. Pierce pursued his dream of flight and never gave up until he converted that desire to reality. Pierce died before I was born and Rose passed on when I was very young; researching this book has allowed me to get to know them better, for which I am appreciative. It is my wish that this book captures the spirit of adventure by which they lived.

Rose and Pierce "Scotty" O'Carroll in the 1950s.

From the Lynch family collection.

Photo by Peter J. Schulz, city photographer. Courtesy of the City of Chicago, Department of Aviation.

While the aircraft in the foreground holds its position prior to takeoff, a jet lifts off from Midway Airport into a clear sky.

✈ Preface: Hangar Stories

Anyone who hangs around an airport knows that pilots like free coffee. At Monarch Air Service, my family's hangar on Central Avenue at Midway Airport, the coffee was hot and available twenty-four hours a day. Because of this, pilots would park their jets on our tarmac, have a cup of joe, and then take on some fuel.

When these pilots sipped their coffee, swapping stories about their profession, I was the kid in the corner, pushing a broom, working summers during high school, listening.

I heard the story told by the deposed Shah of Iran's personal pilot of how he had once flown Henry Kissinger over the Persian Gulf and fallen asleep in the cockpit, snoozing peacefully and awakening before anyone was the wiser. And the account of the attack on a pilot's B-26 bomber squadron by a ME 262, Germany's first jet, in the skies above Germany during World War II. They talked about their heroes, the airmail pilots, who risked their lives flying the mail in open cockpits.

These pilots were trading memories that weren't just personal anecdotes, but examples of their participation in the story of aviation, a camaraderie of men who hurled metal through the air near the speed of sound. In my eyes, they were cool beyond words.

While listening to their stories I pieced together images of Midway Airport's golden years—when it was called "Muny," and presidents, princes, world leaders, and movie stars would stop by as the airport lived up to its slogan, "Crossroads of the World." It was a time when flying was for the privileged few, and large crowds would lean against the fence in front of the old terminal on Cicero Avenue and stare in wonder at the airplanes. On special days, they would see the aviators: Charles Lindbergh in the *Spirit of St. Louis*, air racer and war hero Jimmy Doolittle, and air racer Roscoe Turner, who traveled with a lion cub.

I often went to the library to learn more about Midway's early years. Unfortunately, my research would only turn up snippets of information. I came to realize the story of Midway resided in the memories of the old-time pilots who, with every passing year, weren't getting any younger. Then, I did something about it.

In 1995, with a simple tape recorder in hand, I set out to preserve these oral histories of Midway. I interviewed old-timers and the not-so-old, people with personal connections to the airport. From the many hours of interviews, I have assembled the following narrative. Although each interview was done in a separate time and place, I have combined them so that each chapter unfolds as if the participants were once again swapping stories in the hangar over coffee.

I invite you to grab your own cup of coffee, sit back, and join us for the flight.

—CHRISTOPHER LYNCH
CHICAGO, ILLINOIS

✈ A Note on Oral History and the Interviews

This book was compiled from many hours of interviews. Converting the cadence and other nuances of spoken memories into a flowing written narrative is the tricky task an oral historian faces. In the following chapters, the words of those interviewed are their own. To ensure clarity, pauses, tangents, and repetitive information have been edited out. And, as mentioned previously, separate interviews were spliced together around themes to recreate the feel of pilots sharing their stories. If there are any inaccuracies, they are solely those of the author.

The individuals interviewed are identified with a photograph and a brief biography the first time they appear in the work. From then on, for the sake of smooth transitions, there are times when they'll be identified only by their initials.

Charles Downey, the youngest naval aviator of World War II, has an impressive aviation résumé, ranging from being awarded the Distinguished Flying Cross for assisting in sinking a Japanese cruiser with his Hellfighter in Manila Harbor in 1944, to being one of the early executives that brought Midway Airlines to prominence in the 1980s. Based at Midway Airport with American Airlines from 1952 through to their eventual relocation to O'Hare, Downey's observations on the challenge of Midway Airport to weather those dark days in its history add much to the story of the airport.

Fred Farbin. It was a ride on a Ferris Wheel in 1944 that would change Fred Farbin's life. Fred and a friend found themselves temporarily stopped on top of a Ferris Wheel at a carnival at 63rd and Cicero. As they waited, Fred watched the planes landing at nearby Chicago Municipal Airport and suggested to his friend that they go over and check out the airplanes. The two teenagers crossed the street and saw a sign advertising Monarch sightseeing flights. After buying their tickets, Fred climbed into the cockpit of a Stinson SR-9. The pilot, Pierce "Scotty" O'Carroll, chatted with him a bit and soon asked Fred if he wanted a job. Fred said *yes*, and except for a tour in the Merchant Marines during World War II, Monarch Air Service was his life's work over the next four decades. In 1985, shortly before Farbin's death, the author sat down with him to record an interview about Midway's past. Farbin's comments have been transcribed from that interview.

Philip Felper brought to his interview not only a great enthusiasm for aviation based on half a century of flying, but also tremendous insight into the evolution of Midway Airport. Over the course of a career that began with American Airlines in 1939 and continued on through the flying of corporate jets in the 1980s, Felper amassed a collection of stories that are witty, entertaining, and revealing. He personifies the image of the dashing pilot, one that—to borrow from Tom Wolfe's famous phrase—still has "The Right Stuff."

Thomas W. Goldthorpe ran a flight school, T & G Aviation. An astute commentator on aviation topics, he adds much to the discussion of the age of heroes with his thoughts on such larger-than-life figures as the Wright Brothers, Charles Lindbergh, and Jimmy Doolittle. Goldthorpe's interview covers the sweeping changes that took place in aviation from the launch of the Wright Flyer at Kitty Hawk, North Carolina, to the landing of Neil Armstrong on the Moon. Goldthorpe is also a talented artist who contributed three original drawings for this book.

Phil Henderson. As a young man, Henderson led squadrons of B-26 bombers over German targets in World War II, flying 44 missions in all. Phil is one of the first Americans to see a jet, as a German jet got up close and personal with him as it tried to shoot down his bomber over Germany in the Spring of 1944. Henderson spent his professional life flying corporate jets out of Midway.

Robert Hill is the author of the valuable book, *A Little Known Story of the Land Called Clearing*, which is an exceptional look at the Clearing District and the major role that the airport and aviation had on that area.

Harold Lind is an expert on Chicago's central role in the pioneering days of aviation and the special breed of airmail pilot required to face the dangers of early flying. During his excavations of Checkerboard Field in Maywood—now a forest preserve, but the hub of U.S. airmail flights in 1920—Lind retrieved such artifacts uncovering the old cinder runways as an airspeed indicator from an airmail biplane. Lind spoke of the impact of airmail on Chicago while giving a tour of the green lawns that were once Checkerboard field.

Sheila O'Carroll Lynch provided one of my favorite interviews, but let me state my bias—she is my mom. As a young woman, she flew with her father Pierce "Scotty" O'Carroll, one of the early pilots to fly out of Municipal Airport. He would eventually start Monarch Air Service there.

David M. Young, an historian and retired transportation writer for the *Chicago Tribune,* has written extensively about aviation pioneer Octave Chanute's accomplishments upon the Indiana sand dunes. Young's excellent book, *Fill the Heavens with Commerce* (1981 with Neal Callahan), chronicles Chanute's early attempts at flight. He has also written *Chicago Transit* (1988) and *Chicago Maritime* (2001) and co-written *The Illinois Story* (2001). His *Chicago Aviation: An Illustrated History* is scheduled to be published in Spring 2003.

Chicago's Midway Airport

✈

This will be the gate of empire, this the seat of commerce. Everything invites to action. The typical man who will grow up here must be an enterprising man. Each day as he rises he will exclaim, "I act, I move, I push," and there will be spread before him a boundless horizon, an illimitable field of activity.

—RENÉ-ROBERT CAVELIER, SIEUR DE LA SALLE
The French explorer in a letter written in the winter of 1682–83,
not far from where another field of activity would spring up 244 years later.

It remains a midland portage. No railroad passes through the city. Passengers shift from one to another of half a dozen stations. Freight trains are shunted around belt lines. But the constellations overhead begin to lend it the look of a mid-world portage, with all the sky for its ocean-port.

—NELSON ALGREN
Chicago: City on the Make, 1951

An example of a motorized glider, equipped with pontoons.

✈ INTRODUCTION

BY DAVID M. YOUNG

David M. Young is the former transportation editor of the *Chicago Tribune*, and the author of *Chicago Transit: An Illustrated History*, the first book of a multi-volume series on the history of transportation in Chicago that includes his *Chicago Maritime* (2001) and *Chicago Aviation* (2003). He is also the co-author of *Fill the Heavens with Commerce*, the definitive work on pioneering aviation in Chicago. In this introduction, Young describes the development of Midway Airport over the last 75 years and its critical role in aviation history and Chicago history.

B y the time the City of Chicago got around to building a commercial airport, humans had been flying in heavier-than-air machines for nearly a quarter of a century and aviation was well established. Within a few years of the new airport's opening, however, it was one of the busiest in the world, if not, as local boosters claimed, the world's busiest, a position it would hold through the middle of the twentieth century. Then it yielded its title, but only to a new airport built on the other side of town. The transportation crossroads of Chicago, it seems, was as difficult for the aviation industry to avoid in the twentieth century as it had been for the creaking schooners, plodding canal boats, and puffing steam locomotives in the nineteenth.

Geography endowed Chicago with a unique position in the center of the North American continent, the place where the watersheds of the Great Lakes and Mississippi River approach within a few miles of each other. Watersheds were critical to early commercial transport even after the railroads came along because they provided relatively level transportation corridors for steamboats and steam engines alike.

The city, a canoe portage and perhaps a fortified outpost in French colonial times, in the nineteenth century attained a critical mass that commercial land and sea transport found increasingly hard to bypass. It was perhaps because of the synergy between sea and land transport—the Great Lakes, rivers, canals, and railroads—that Chicago attained critical mass and became the mid-continental transportation nexus; the synergy certainly offered options to passengers and shippers alike and served to control rates. For many of the same reasons, commercial airplanes, when they finally appeared in the 1920s, were able to leap the Great Lakes and mountain ranges but not the Loop.

The seminal year in commercial aviation, if there was such a benchmark, was probably 1918 when thousands of daring young men who learned to fly for the Army and their machines suddenly became avail-

From the Lynch family collection.

A later model of the many types of aircraft manufactured
by Glenn Curtiss, one of the main rivals of the Wright brothers.

able for other pursuits when the Armistice concluded World War I. That was also the year the U.S. Post Office Department began flying mail on a regular basis.

Prior to World War I, aviation had been a sport; indeed, the only money to be made was from manufacturing and exhibiting flying machines. The brothers Orville and Wilbur Wright and their principal American rival, Glenn Curtiss, designed and built aircraft, taught young daredevils how to fly them, and assembled teams of aviators to demonstrate them before huge crowds at air shows and county fairs

across the nation. Despite the fact that the venerable Chicago aviation pioneer Octave Chanute had given considerable advice and encouragement to the Wrights prior to their successful experiments near Kitty Hawk in 1903, the first flight of a heavier-than-air machine over the Chicago area didn't occur until 1909 when Curtiss showed up to give a demonstration at the Hawthorne Race Track in west suburban Cicero. The following year the Wrights sent pioneer pilot Walter P. Brookins to Chicago to win a $10,000 prize offered by the *Chicago Record Herald* for a flight between the Windy City and Springfield.

During the 1911 Air Show in Chicago's Grant Park, Briton T.O.M. Sopwith won $14,020 in prize money; Lincoln Beachey, flying for Curtiss, won $11,667; and C.P. Rodgers on the Wright team won $11,285. The prizes won by the top aviators were considerable sums of money at that time, but the cities able to afford such aerial extravaganzas were relatively rare, so many barnstormers earned pocket money by giving rides on their machines at county fairs to anyone who could afford $5. It was an industry, like ballooning before it, that had very limited economic possibilities.

As a result, the need for flying fields was minimal. The extravaganzas could be staged in large urban parks, as was the 1911 Chicago Air Show in Grant Park, or at race tracks like the New York Air Show at Belmont Park the prior year. A farm pasture with a shed could serve as a permanent base for airplanes, and that was what the Wrights used in Dayton for a while. James E. Plew, Curtiss's airplane dealer in

Chicago, in 1910 had a similar arrangement at 65th Street and Major Avenue not far from where Midway Airport eventually would rise. At that time the only other aviation center in Chicago that could be considered permanent was the balloon and blimp port and adjacent air strip at White City Amusement Park, 63rd Street and South Parkway.

The metropolitan area's first permanent facility that can be described as an airport in the modern sense of the word was established in 1911 in suburban Cicero to handle the activities of the Aero Club of Illinois, a group of wealthy aviation buffs and flying enthusiasts. For a time before World War I, Cicero Field was perhaps the busiest airport in the world and acted as a magnet for young men and women from around the nation who wanted to learn to fly. Katherine Stinson began her flying career there, and such eventual aviation giants as Chance Vought and Glen Martin passed through Cicero Field early in their careers.

Cicero Field was succeeded just before World War I by Ashburn Field, the Aero Club's new airport at 83rd Street and Cicero Avenue. It proved, however, to be too marshy to handle the heavier aircraft coming off the production lines during the war, and the federal government was forced to build its new air base named after Chanute at Rantoul in central Illinois. The federal Air Mail Service which began in 1918 using military planes and pilots chose Grant Park as its airfield.

Although there had been fleeting attempts to organize airlines and air freight services earlier, the Air Mail Service was the beginning of commercial aviation in the United States. Continuous commercial air service dates from that government airline organized by former Chicagoan Benjamin Lipsner, a professional manager, not a flier, who had his first brush with aviation at Plew's airport at 65th and Major a few years earlier. The decision by Congress to transfer the carrying of mail from the government airline to private carriers in 1925 led directly to the creation of the U.S. airline industry a year later.

In 1918, Lipsner selected Grant Park as the Chicago base for the fledgling Air Mail Service primarily because there was plenty of open space and it was near the Loop, but it was an untenable compromise. Conservationists who wanted the land kept as a park might have been willing to accept the airport as a wartime compromise, but once peace resumed they renewed their campaign to protect the city's downtown lakefront. The Wingfoot Air Express disaster in the Loop the following year sealed Grant Park's fate.

The Wingfoot was the Goodyear Tire and Rubber Company's first commercial blimp, and on June 29, 1919, following some public demonstration flights from Grant Park, the airship lifted off for its return trip to its base at White City. It caught fire, however, while passing over the Loop and crashed through the skylight of the Illinois Trust and Savings Bank at LaSalle Street and Jackson Boulevard. Thirteen persons, including ten bank employees, died in the crash and resulting explosion on the bank's main business floor.

Katherine Stinson, an early aviator, learned how to fly in Chicago in 1912 and would go on to be a stunt flyer at air shows.

The Post Office moved its Chicago airmail operations to Checkerboard Field, a small airport at 12th Street (Roosevelt Road) and First Avenue in suburban Maywood in 1920, and after a fire there a few years later moved again to adjacent Maywood Field. Maywood became the Chicago base for most airlines when they came into existence in 1926, although a joint venture between William B. Stout and Henry Ford resulted in freight service between Detroit and south suburban Lansing beginning April 3, 1925, with single-engine Ford AT-2 aircraft built by Stout. Charles A. Lindbergh, the pilot who later became famous for making the first solo transatlantic crossing by airplane, is popularly, though incorrectly, credited with commencing scheduled commercial airline service in the Chicago area on April 15, 1926, when he flew between St. Louis and Maywood.

Meanwhile, Chicago was not entirely oblivious to the necessity of having a commercial airport, primarily because Charles Dickinson, a wealthy seed company owner, and the Aero Club of Chicago lobbied the city for additional airports to promote the pastime of flying and augment the club's Ashburn Field. He convinced Mayor William Hale Thompson of the need, and the city on October 1, 1922, officially opened a small flying field on a portion of a square mile of open land at Cicero Avenue and 63rd Street. It was a modest beginning for what would eventually become the world's busiest airport, and for its first few years was used primarily as a practice field by pilots based at Ashburn and Maywood.

A few weeks after the Post Office in 1924 began round-the-clock airmail service over its transcontinental route between New York and San Francisco via Chicago (actually suburban Maywood), Charles H. Wacker, the influential chairman of the Chicago Plan Commission, urged Chicago to establish an all-weather municipal landing field. The City Council before the end of the year unanimously adopted a resolution to have its Committee on Public Works and Recreation find a site for a municipal airport.

Nothing was done, however, until Emil (Matty) Laird, a local airplane builder, in March, 1925, asked to lease the airport at 63rd Street and Cicero Avenue so he could build an aircraft factory there. A month earlier President Calvin Coolidge had signed the Kelly Act, turning over the hauling of air mail from the Post Office to private carriers. It was obvious to the city's leaders that a municipal airport was inevitable, and the City Council soon after Laird made his request adopted an ordinance authorizing the city to negotiate with the Chicago Board of Education to permanently lease the 63rd and Cicero site for an

Courtesy of David M. Young.

Alfred O. Sporrer (left) and Charles Dickenson (center), with Emil (Matty) Laird, an airplane manufacturer whose factory was on the South Side of Chicago.

Alfred O. Sporrer in the cockpit of an airmail plane at Ashburn Field, 1926.

airport.

The new and as yet uncompleted field was dedicated on May 8, 1926, with a ceremony that included a flight by one of the new airlines, National Air Transport. After the festivities, the NAT plane returned to Maywood from where it inaugurated airmail service to Dallas four days later. NAT, as a result of a series of mergers a few years later, became United Air Lines. The 120-acre Municipal Airport, as it was then called, returned to its sleepy existence as a practice field until its cinder runways, the longest of which was 3,600 feet, were completed. The airlines then shifted their operations there from Maywood on December 1, 1927—the date the City of Chicago

claims is the official opening of the airport.

Municipal Airport in its early years was primarily an airmail facility; only 15,498 passengers used the airport's 41,660 flights in its first full year of operation in 1928. By 1930 there was still an average of only about one person per flight. In fact, NAT in its early years discouraged passengers, and Municipal Airport didn't even have a passenger terminal until 1931. Relatively high air fares of the day, the public's fear of flying, the relatively small size of early commercial aircraft, strong competition from the railroads, which modernized their fleets with streamliners, and the Great Depression also combined to keep the number of air passengers below what they might otherwise have been. Nevertheless, 700,000 people flew in and out of Chicago's airport in 1940, and despite wartime restrictions on civilian travel, Municipal served more than a million passengers in 1944.

As early as 1936, the airlines were warning that the airport needed to be expanded if it was expected to be able to handle the four-engine aircraft that were expected to take to the air within a few years. At the time, the 21-passenger, twin-engine DC-3 was the hottest commercial plane flying. Chicago, concerned that the airlines would bypass the city if Municipal Airport couldn't handle the four-engine planes, almost immediately embarked on an $8.5-million program to more than double the airport in size. A railroad was relocated to create a mile-square site that would accommodate the necessary 5,000-foot-long runways. In 1942 the City Council voted to build a new terminal for $1.2 million.

was in an undeveloped area of the city, but as aviation became a more acceptable method of transportation, the mile-square airport became ringed by all sorts of businesses, industries, aviation-related offices, and, finally, housing subdivisions. That made expanding the airport a very expensive proposition, especially since the city could obtain for almost nothing the site of O'Hare for a larger airport.

The second factor working against Midway was the rapid growth in the size of aircraft. After World War II, the ubiquitous, 21-seat DC-3s were rapidly supplanted by war-surplus C-54s, a four-engine aircraft with more than double the number of seats of its predecessor. The C-54, which in civil aviation was known as the DC-4, in turn was replaced by even larger DC-6s and DC-7s and Lockheed Super Constellations, but the primary concern of aviation plan-

Courtesy of Dean Del Bene.

In the 1930s, as airlines branched out to serve more cities, new routes would be charted by a route survey plane, like this one for American Airways. The route survey would ensure that alternate landing sites along the flight path were acceptable.

That was the same year that Douglas Aircraft Company began expanding Orchard Place Airport near northwest suburban Park Ridge to accommodate a factory to build four-engine C-54 transports for World War II. Orchard-Douglas Airport (ORD in the code used by the airlines to identify airports) eventually became O'Hare International Airport and superseded Midway as the world's busiest. Municipal itself was renamed Midway in 1949.

Midway's success as an airport was its own eventual undoing. Its site was originally chosen because it

A Wisconsin Central DC-3 parked at Midway Airport in 1951. First introduced by the airlines in 1936, the DC-3 was a reliable ship that revolutionized commercial aviation and flew commercially for years. It could carry 21 passengers.

Courtesy of Robert F. Soraparu.

Courtesy of Robert F. Soraparu.

A United Air Lines DC-4 at Chicago Municipal Airport (Midway) in 1947.

were making their appearances, but the airport was jammed to capacity on the ground and in the air.

Then the airlines began shifting their traffic to the new O'Hare Airport, and by 1963 what had been the world's busiest airport just four years earlier was reduced to the status of a ghost town with only 126,959 flights, most of them by general aviation and corporate aircraft, carrying 417,544 passengers. The reasons for Midway's abrupt decline had as much to do with airline economics as it did the inadequacy of the older airport's runways to handle the jets of the time. The airlines did not want to pay for duplicate facilities, and Chicago's role as a connecting center mitigated against two hub airports. As many as half the passengers passing through O'Hare were simply changing airplanes.

Mayor Richard J. Daley in the late 1960s began lobbying the airlines to transfer some flights back to Midway, and the airlines acquiesced. The Midway service, however, was for the most part additional service, not flights transferred there from O'Hare. The annual number of flights at Midway increased by 42,000 between 1965 and 1966, but they increased by 34,000 at O'Hare over the same span. By 1971 Midway had undergone a modest revival and was handling nearly 2 million passengers, but O'Hare that year handled 30 million.

Traffic at Midway collapsed once again after 1973 when the world oil crises caused a rapid increase in the price of jet fuel; the airlines got caught with too many large jets in their fleets, resulting in too many unfilled seats; and the carriers cut back on flights to

ners was the development of commercial jet aircraft.

The original British Comet jetliner introduced in 1952 was not much larger than the propeller-driven aircraft of that era, but the Boeing 707s and Douglas DC-8s that followed it were considerably larger, and equally important from the standpoint of America's airports, and required substantially longer runways, not to mention more spacious terminals to handle all the people occupying the extra seats. Midway passenger traffic peaked at 431,400 flights and more than 10 million passengers in 1959 just as the big new jets

Chicago Midway Airport in the 1950s, when it was the world's busiest airport.

Commercial aviation moved from Midway to O'Hare in 1962. One of the advantages of O'Hare was its extended runways that could handle the larger jets, such as the Boeing 707 and later the 747. Midway Airport's longest runway, even at a mile long, was too short for those jets.

save money. The number of flights annually at Midway declined by 27,000 between 1971 and 1976, and passenger traffic dropped to 547,000—slightly more than a third of what it had been in 1971. Midway was once again a ghost town.

Relief finally came in the form of airline deregulation that not only permitted established intrastate carriers in places like Florida, Texas, and California to expand beyond those states' borders but entirely new carriers to enter the market. Before that, the Civil Aeronautics Board had tightly regulated airline routes, ostensibly to keep the industry healthy by preventing predatory competition. The first entirely new post-deregulation airline to emerge in the United States was formed by a group of aviation entrepreneurs and venture capitalists and was named Midway after the airport that was its hub of operations.

Midway's strategy was to operate a budget airline by flying relatively inexpensive used jets and charging fares substantially below what the trunk airlines at O'Hare charged. The new carrier's effect on Midway Airport traffic was dramatic. Although the new airline survived only twelve years, it was to a large extent responsible for an eight-fold increase in passengers using the South Side airport for which it was named. Aircraft operations (flights) at the airport jumped from just under 190,000 in 1979, when Midway Airlines went into operation, to 320,000 in 1989, and passenger traffic over the same span swelled to 8.5 million from 896,000.

Although Midway Airlines filed for bankruptcy

Courtesy of the City of Chicago, Department of Aviation.

A Midway Airlines DC-9 prepares to take off, while another holds in position, 1980s.

and was liquidated in 1991, causing traffic to fall to less than half of what it had been before the airline failed, Chicago officials talked Southwest Airlines into filling the gap. Southwest was a former intrastate airline that as a deregulated budget carrier had successfully been able to compete with the trunks. The entry of Southwest and other budget carriers caused Midway Airport traffic to increase once again. The city responded by building a rapid transit line to the airport, modernizing and expanding its terminals, and adding huge parking lots. Passengers who 20 years earlier parked in a lot a few feet in front of the main terminal entrance to catch a rare flight, by the late 1990s had to park in remote lots north of 55th Street and be hauled by shuttle bus to their gates.

By 1998, the airport set a new record for passenger traffic—11.4 million—topping the old record of

10,040,353 set in 1959 when it was still the world's busiest airport. By the end of the century, Midway was handling nearly 15.7 million passengers, although by then traffic at O'Hare had grown to 72 million, and officials of the State of Illinois were promoting the construction of a south suburban airport to relieve aerial congestion.

✈

Courtesy of the City of Chicago, Department of Aviation.

Southwest Airlines jets parked at the terminal
at Chicago Midway Airport, early 1990s.

Part I

From Miller Beach to Municipal Airport
1896–1926

✈

Let us hope that the advent of a successful flying machine, now only dimly foreseen and nevertheless thought to be possible, will bring nothing but good into the world; that it shall abridge distance, make all parts of the globe accessible, bring men into closer relation with each other, advance civilization, and hasten the promised era in which there shall be nothing but peace and good-will among men.[1]

—OCTAVE CHANUTE
Progress in Flying Machines, 1894

If he had not lived, the entire history of progress in flying would have been other than it has been . . . His writings were so lucid as to provide an intelligent understanding of the nature of the problems of flight to a vast number of persons who would probably never have given the matter study otherwise, and not only by published articles, but by personal correspondence and visitation, he inspired and encouraged to the limits of his ability all who were devoted to the work. His private correspondence with experimenters in all parts of the world was of great volume. No one was too humble to receive a share of his time. In patience and goodness of heart he has rarely been surpassed. Few men were more universally respected and loved.[2]

—WILBUR WRIGHT
Tribute to Octave Chanute, published in
Aeronautics magazine after Chanute's death in 1910.

Octave Chanute, a Chicago Railway engineer whose experiments with gliders at Miller Beach in Northwest Indiana would inspire the Wright Brothers.

Drawing by Thomas W. Goldthorpe.

✈ THE DREAMERS

Midway Airport has been a mirror of Chicago for more than seventy-five years. When Chicago roared in the 1920s, the Southwest Side field became the city's first official airport. Over the next few decades, it was the busiest airport in the nation, and then the world.

The airport would become a hub of transportation for commercial aviation in the twentieth century just as Chicago had been a railroad hub during the nineteenth century. Midway's success would ultimately lead to its decline, with houses, restaurants, and hotels blocking any possible expansion needed for the jet age.

During lean economic years, the airport would lay fallow, like the farmer's field it once had been. Yet in the late 1970s, when entrepreneurs decided to create Midway Airlines, the airport would be rediscovered.

Midway's story is a tale of heroes and villains, generosity and greed, boom and bust, progress,

decline, and ultimately success. The airport's origins reach back to the dawn of human flight, and this narrative will explore its legacy, a great American story in danger of being forgotten.

A few miles southeast of Midway, as the crow flies, is the spot where the saga began, on the sandy dunes of Miller Beach, on the shores of what is now Gary, Indiana.

Today only sea gulls fly where once Octave Chanute, a French-born engineer, dreamed of soaring above the sand dunes. It was at Miller Beach that Chanute built and launched elaborate kites in 1896 as he chased the dream of flight, a quest sought continuously since ancient history, from the mythological attempts of Icarus and Daedalus to the experiments in the Renaissance by Leonardo da Vinci. And on the eve of the twentieth century, it would be Chanute's turn to try to unlock the elusive secret of flight.

As David M. Young wrote in the introduction to

The U.S. Post Office celebrated Octave Chanute's glider experiments with a stamp in his honor and this commemorative envelope.

this book, Octave Chanute's experiments would have a profound influence on the study of flight in the late nineteenth and early twentieth centuries. "Chanute is one of the most interesting people in aviation history. He was a railroad engineer, and by this I don't mean he drove the trains; he built the bridges and laid out the railroads. He built much of the Santa Fe Railroad and the old Chicago and Alton Railroad, which is now the line on which Amtrak runs down through Joliet to St. Louis.

"Somewhere in his career Chanute became interested in the possibility of flying. There were no airplanes. The only flight was by balloons. Hot air balloons were popular. Hydrogen was used as a fuel but was very dangerous. Not only did it catch on fire from time to time, but tended to become uncontrollable. You might rocket into the stratosphere in a balloon, and that happened a few times.

"Chanute was not so much an inventor as he was an accumulator of knowledge, reading all there was on heavier-than-air machines in the 1880s and 1890s and assembling it in a book entitled *Progress in Flying Machines*. Deciding that wasn't enough, he began to test glider apparatus which today we would call airframes. The lead experimenter at the time was Lilienthal in Germany, while Langley was working on it in Washington.

"In summer 1896, Chanute and some of his associates, including Augustus Herring, went to Miller Beach because of its favorable winds and sand dunes from which they could jump and land and not risk injury. They jumped and landed in some of the most incredible-looking devices you've ever seen, including a huge bat-like contraption invented by a man named Beudiscoffen.

"Not being entirely satisfied with the results, Chanute resumed his experimentation back in Chicago, and what emerged from this second round was a Pratt truss biplane, which wasn't a plane at all, but a glider. This seemed to be the most successful of the airframes that he developed. The big problem was how to control it in flight. In a hang glider, as we call them today,

Photo by the author.

The Wright memorial on Big Kill Devil Hill on the Outer Banks of North Carolina.

which was really what Chanute was using, you would try to gain control by twisting your body around. People had thought of it, but had not put it on a plane. Vertical stabilizers, horizontal stabilizers, and ailerons—three-axis control—had been conceived of but not applied to flight.

"After Chanute published the results of his glider experiments he received a letter from a couple of brothers in Dayton, Ohio, named Wright, who were also working on gliders and were interested in learning more and where the most favorable winds were. Chanute suggested San Diego and the Outer Islands of North Carolina. The trio became good friends, and the Wrights visited Chanute in Chicago."

"At this point the Wrights were learning more from Chanute," states Thomas W. Goldthorpe, "but the roles of mentor and student reversed quickly once the Wrights began their experiments and far surpassed anything that Chanute was doing."

"Chanute was in North Carolina in 1903 when the Wrights were getting ready to do flight trials. Unfortunately he was getting up in years and when the weather turned bad he was forced to leave, missing the Wrights' first flight." [DY]

Thomas W. Goldthorpe is a pilot who owned and operated a flight school out of Midway Airport, T & G Aviation, which he sold in the mid-1990s. An astute commentator on aviation topics, he adds much to the discussion of the age of heroes with his thoughts on such larger-than-life figures as the Wright Brothers, Charles Lindbergh, and Jimmy Doolittle. Goldthorpe's interview covers the sweeping changes that took place in aviation from the launch of the Wright Flyer at Kitty Hawk, North Carolina, to the landing of Neil Armstrong on the Moon. Goldthorpe is also a talented artist who contributed three drawings to this book.

WRIGHT FLYER 1

Drawing by Thomas W. Goldthorpe.

The Wright Flyer.

Chanute was in his Chicago home at 1138 N. Dearborn Street on December 17, when he received a telegram from the Wrights' sister, Katharine, which simply read, 'The boys have done it.' The age of controlled flight was born.[4]

"Winning a coin toss, Wilbur was the first to make the flight attempt. He got up in the air and flew about 100 feet. But due to design and structural problems the airplane pitched sharply right after it zoomed out of its launch rails. Wilbur overcompensated with the elevator by pitching it down, and the airplane smacked into the sand, damaging the elevator and the landing skids.

"Three days later, on December 17, having been delayed by poor weather and repairs, Orville tried flight a second time. He climbed onto the machine

Several men prepare a motorized glider on a frozen lake, one of the many prototypes of aircraft inspired by the Wright brothers' famous flight in 1903.

From the Lynch family collection.

A motorized
glider in flight.

with the wind blowing about 27 miles an hour, Wilbur cranked up, and Orville took off after a run of about 60 feet. He flew 120 feet and landed. Being scrupulously honest with themselves, they wouldn't accept Wilbur's first attempt three days earlier as a flight.

"Chanute didn't really appreciate how the Wrights accomplished the first flight being unable to grasp the three-axis control." [TG]

"There was not much aeronautical activity in Chicago after Chanute's glider experiments, until 1909—one reason being the secretiveness of the Wrights about their invention resulting from their struggle to gain patent rights for the plane." [DY] "This was partly the Wrights' fault," Goldthorpe points out, "in that they didn't have a patent on their

A photograph of Glenn Curtiss (left) and Henry Ford. Curtiss, an early rival of the Wright Brothers, was the first person to fly in the Chicago area, in an exhibition flight at Hawthorne Race Track in Cicero, Illinois, on October 16, 1909.

BROOKINS IN HIS AEROPLANE, OVER CHICAGO YACHT CLUB HOUSE AND GRANT PARK, CHICAGO

From the author's collection.

A postcard showing Walter Brookins flying over Grant Park and the Illinois Central Railway tracks in 1910. Brookins's flight was the first recorded flight over Chicago proper; Glenn Curtiss's flight in 1909 took place in suburban Cicero.

wing-warping process. You see, they didn't really invent the airplane; flight had been accomplished before them. What they eventually patented was the three-axis control system still being used on airplanes today."

David Young continues: "Finally, a group of people who were interested in aviation got Glen Curtiss to come to Chicago and do a flight at Hawthorne Race Track, after which they formed the Aero Club of Illinois to promote aviation and essentially began Chicago aviation history. In those days only the wealthy owned motor cars and could afford airplanes. Chanute remained the first club president until his death in 1910.

"Once the club was formed, people like the McCormick family (both International Harvester and *Chicago Tribune* sides) and Charles "Pops" Dickenson, who owned a seed company, became involved. They then began not so much to build and develop airplanes on their own, although there was a little bit of that going on in Chicago, but to promote events to interest the public in aviation.

"Grant Park and other fields were being used occasionally as an airport, but wanting a permanent venue for the Aero Club, the McCormick family donated land they owned in Cicero to be used as Cicero Field, the first permanent airport."

"In 1911 a spectacular air show was held in Chicago. Hundreds of thousands of people came to see these flying machines, the first mass public exposure to aviation. The idea of human flight was a novelty; the notion prevailed that had God intended man to fly he would have given him wings. They had to see it with their own eyes to believe it." [TG]

"Virtually everybody in aviation in the United States and a number of people from England came to the 1911 aerial show in Grant Park. Lincoln Beachey set a world altitude record of over 11,000 feet. He took his airplane, a frame with a wing and a pusher engine, and simply climbed to the highest altitude he could get before his gas ran out, and then he coasted back to the ground.

"Early seaplanes, stunt flying, events with prizes, made up the show's program. Can you imagine a show like this today in Grant Park, with crowds close

A postcard from the 1911 International Aviation Meet, held in Chicago's Grant Park, one of the most spectacular aviation events of its day.

From the author's collection.

INTERNATIONAL AVIATION MEET CHICAGO 1911

Lincoln Beachey, who set a world altitude record of 11,642 feet in 1911 at the International Aviation Meet in Chicago.

to the runways and kids running out in front of the planes? Despite the danger, the 1911 air show whetted the public's appetite for aviation and was a great success despite a few deaths from air crashes.

"The show attracted the Wright brothers whose reason for coming was less for the spectacle than for assurance that their patents would be protected. The Aero Club had to reach a settlement with them at the eleventh hour for the show to go on because technically they had the only patent that existed regarding an airplane, and at the show you had all kinds of people flying aircraft that weren't Wright flyers. It is purported the club had to make a cash settlement to mollify the Wrights and protect their patent." [DY]

"The brothers, especially Wilbur, were adamant

A view of the 1911 International Aviation Meet held in Chicago's Grant Park. The Chicago Yacht Club is visible in the background.

about defending their patents and would religiously take anyone to court who attempted infringement. He was disliked for this and regarded as excessively greedy. This view is not quite understandable when one considers that Edison and Bell, both great inventors, defended the patents on their inventions, became immensely wealthy, and became enshrined as American folk heroes and great inventors. The Wrights were doing the same thing, no more, no less. They were probably hated because an airplane was something that gave man the ability to fly like gods." [TG]

Shortly after, Chicago would again become the center of the aviation world as host of the Gordon Bennett Cup Races. The 1911 race was won by American C. T. Weymann in Eastchurch, England,

STONE STARTING TRIP ENDING IN ACCIDENT SAT. AUG. 12.
INTERNATIONAL AVIATION MEET CHICAGO AUGUST 1911

WRECK OF STONE'S MONOPLANE INTERNATIONAL AVIATION MEET CHICAGO 1911

and according to tradition, this allowed the winner's country to host the next year's race. The Aero Club of Illinois lost little time in petitioning for the race to be held in Illinois. And so, in 1912, the best fliers in the world once again descended upon Chicago to compete in the worldwide race in tribute to the Club, the premier aviation outfit in the United States.[5]

The race was first scheduled to be flown over Grant Park. Part of the course was to be over Lake Michigan, but the organizers and pilots did not want to fly over water. Instead the race course was set around 73rd Street and Central Avenue.

"The race was rather disappointing; it was not nearly as spectacular as the air show because it consisted of just a bunch of planes flying around in circles. It increased the public's appetite for aviation, however," Goldthorpe observes. "Flying was still

Above: Arthur Stone and a passenger prepare to take off in Stone's Queen Bleriot monoplane at the International Aviation Meet in Grant Park, 1911.
Left: Stone's monoplane after a crash at the International Aviation Meet in Grant Park, 1911. No one was injured.

Courtesy of Joshua Koppel.

interested in flying, the role of Chicago's aviation benefactor would rest with Charles Dickenson. He was a third generation capitalist with a Quaker background that instilled in him a sense of social responsibility. Employees of his seed company were not only provided with free meals, but were also eligible for interest-free loans for buying homes. At the age of 70 Dickenson soloed his first aircraft, and he would now keep the dream of flight alive in Chicago. His first priority would be to find a flying field in the city.[6]

"As World War I was underway, Dickenson decided the only way Chicago was going to have an airport was if he bought land and donated it to the Aero Club. He bought some open farm land about a mile and a half from where Midway Airport is today. The airport was called Ashburn Field.

"Dickenson donated the land and a tower was built, probably the earliest attempt to control traffic at an airport, at least at a Chicago airport. They must have used hand signals because planes didn't have radios.

"Ashburn Field's runways were 2,500 feet long and a little shorter in one direction than the other. They were soft and unpaved so pilots had to be very careful. At that time the poorly engineered planes often developed engine trouble causing many accidents." [DY]

Philip Felper recalls that he checked out [took his first solo flight] at Ashburn Field in a plane "with no brakes—a Buell Bull Pup with an ancient three-cylinder Szekely engine with a cable around the cylinders because every so often one would pop off

Courtesy of David M. Young.

Charles Dickenson, the successful businessman who was an early proponent of aviation in Chicago.

considered a fad and an amusement."

As the McCormick family became less and less

Philip Felper
brought to his interview not only a great enthusiasm for aviation based on half a century of flying, but also tremendous insight into the evolution of Midway Airport. Over the course of a career that began with American Airlines in 1939 and continued on through the flying of corporate jets in the 1980s, Felper amassed a collection of stories that are witty, entertaining, and revealing. He personifies the image of the dashing pilot; one that—to borrow from Tom Wolfe's famous phrase—still has "The Right Stuff."

and the cable kept it from hitting you in the head. The plane was open cockpit, so you wore a helmet and goggles. There was no oil feed to engines in those early days so you had to grease them. And as you flew, the grease would shoot out onto your goggles and you ended up half-blind.

"With no brakes, I had to plan—once, twice, three times around to find a speed that would enable me to land safely. My airplane had no airspeed indicator so I had to guess. It took me three times one Sunday to get up, around, and land. The first time I knew I was too fast; the second time I knew I was too fast; the third time I thought I could make it; if I didn't, I would go into a ditch.

"I made it the third time, dug my skid in, landed, and held. I remember that everybody on the field was waiting for me to get killed! I pulled up in front of them, got out of the airplane, strutted around, and said: 'I's a pilot! I's a pilot!'"

While Charles Dickenson had donated the land to create Ashburn Field, and in so doing, gave pilots a chance to fly in the Chicago area, he was also trying to demonstrate to the city the benefits of aviation.

In 1929, Dickenson donated 65 acres of land in

An LCB-3000 aircraft at Ashburn Field at 83rd and Cicero, one of the first airfields established in Chicago.

Courtesy of Robert F. Zilinsky.

the Lake Calumet region to the city suggesting it be used as an airport and a seaplane base. The City Council was thankful but unsure about what to do with the property. Ironically, 60 years later, the city would propose Lake Calumet as the site of a third airport.[7]

✈

1. Octave Chanute, *Progress in Flying Machines* (Long Beach, CA: Lorenz & Herwig, 1977).

2. Stephen Kirk, *First in Flight: The Wright Brothers in North Carolina* (Winston Salem, NC: John F. Blair Publisher, 1995), 284.

3. Ibid., 24.

4. David M. Young and Neal Callahan, *Fill the Heavens with Commerce: Chicago Aviation, 1855–1926* (Chicago: Chicago Review Press, 1981), 16.

5. Ibid., 60.

6. Ibid., 89.

7. Ibid., 90.

From the Lynch family collection.

Rose O'Carroll, the author's grandmother (left), and a friend pose in front of an airplane at Ashburn Field in the early 1930s.

Courtesy of the City of Chicago, Department Of Aviation.

Mail being loaded onto a National Air Transport (NAT) airplane in Ohio. The fledgling airlines relied on flying the mail for revenue. The seriousness with which they took this endeavor is evidenced by the man to the left with the shotgun.

✈ FLYING THE MAIL

In the early years of aviation, balloons and blimps were very much a part of the Chicago public's conception of flight possibilities. In fact, blimps were built on the South Side at White City Amusement Park, then located at 63rd Street and South Parkway. It was from there that the Wingfoot, a large airship that carried several passengers, began an ill-fated flight one day in 1919 that almost doomed aviation from progressing in Chicago.

Goodyear, which had been making blimps mainly for the U.S. Navy, was excited by the future of the Wingfoot, its first commercial blimp. It was large, filling approximately 95,000 cubic feet with hydrogen.

July 21, 1919, was the Wingfoot's maiden flight. Its pilot, John Boettner, climbed aboard with his two mechanics and two passengers. They flew first to Grant Park where they were well-received by excited crowds. Then, while over the Loop, the blimp became engulfed in flames, fell uncontrolled towards LaSalle Street and Jackson Boulevard, and smashed through the skylight of the Illinois Trust and Savings Bank where several bank employees were working after hours. Ten banks workers were killed and 28 injured when the flaming Wingfoot crashed to the floor. Three of the Wingfoot's passengers also perished. It was at the time the worst disaster in aviation history.

City officials were outraged. The Cook County State's Attorney's office arrested not only the pilot but several Goodyear executives on possible murder charges. An emergency City Council meeting was called where alderman Anton Cermak, who would later become mayor, drafted an ordinance that would give the city power to regulate all flights over its business sector. Cermak commented at the time that "this accident shows we must stop flying over the city sooner or later, and we better do it sooner."[1]

Other issues soon occupied the City Council's attention, and the matter of flying over the city was shelved. The legacy of the Wingfoot disaster would have a chilling effect on local attitudes towards aviation for years to come and was the main reason that Grant Park was never again used as an airfield.

U.S. soldiers walk in front of several de Havilland "Flying Coffins."

From the author's collection.

A hole scars the skylight where the flaming wreckage of the Wingfoot blimp plummeted, killing ten employees of the Illinois Trust and Savings Bank. This photo, taken immediately after the crash, shows that the building's roof is still on fire.

Courtesy of the City of Chicago, Municipal Reference Collection.

✈ **1918**

World War I ends, and the U.S. army finds itself with a surplus of planes, the de Havilland "Flying Coffins" as they're known by the pilots who fly them. In 1921, the U.S. Post Office would create a program as ambitious as the Pony Express and put these extra planes to use: they would fly the mail from New York to San Francisco. In this new venture, Chicago becomes the hub of the air mail, as it had become the hub of the railroads a century before. Mail is flown into Grant Park on the Chicago's lakefront.

✈ **1919**

City Council is reluctant to allow more flights over the Loop after the Wingfoot disaster, and Grant Park ceases to be used as an airport. The Post Office moves its operation to Checkerboard Field in Maywood the following year.

At first, flying the mail was no way to compete with mail delivered by trains. Too many flights were grounded due to poor visibility and dangerous airplanes. The pilots flew with no radios or proper instruments and often judged their airspeed by the hum of the wires caused by the air flowing between the wings. Flying the mail was an almost suicidal business, and the pilots who did it were courageous, or foolish, depending on your perspective. The routes they forged are littered with their crashed planes and comrades who would never fly again.[2]

David Young: "The Wingfoot was built at White City, a Chicago South Side amusement park that had a hangar for balloon enthusiasts, because the manufacturer had no facilities in Akron. Then, during World War I, Goodyear built a hangar in Akron and shifted wartime production. After the war, Akron was still involved in military production, so Goodyear built their first post-war commercial blimp, called the Wingfoot Air Express because the winged foot was the company's logo, back at White City.

"They did a publicity trip with the blimp—which was inflated with hydrogen—flew to Grant Park, picked up some passengers, took them over the lake, back to Grant Park, and then decided they had better get back to White City.

"One of the photographers on board wanted to get some aerial shots of downtown Chicago so they agreed to take a slight detour over the Loop, let him get his shots, and then return to White City.

"The balloon caught fire over the Loop, crashed through the skylight of a bank just after closing, and exploded when it hit the floor. Twelve or 13 passengers were killed [ten bank employees and three Wingfoot passengers]. No commercial airplane [of the day] would be able to get off the ground carrying that many people.

"The tragedy caused Goodyear to switch from hydrogen to helium to inflate their blimps. The Germans either never learned or couldn't get helium. The Hindenburg disaster twenty years later was proof that hydrogen was a failure as an inflater of lighter-than-air ships.

"The Air Mail Service really wanted to put the Chicago airport in Grant Park, but after the Loop crash the City Council couldn't be persuaded to do so. That's why the Air Mail Service chose Maywood as its site.

"The U.S. Post Office over the years had always experimented with faster ways to carry the mail. In stagecoach days, it was the Pony Express. They were a big factor in railroad development because they moved mail off the steamboats, which were pretty slow, and onto the railroads, which were a lot faster. To a large extent, the highway program in the United States traces its history to the desire of Congress and

Another airmail route is christened. Since the aircraft that flew the mail could only fly short distances, Chicago became a hub for airmail hops.

Courtesy of the City of Chicago, Department of Aviation.

✈ **1921**

Bessie Coleman performs aerobatics at Checkerboard Field in Maywood. In an era when women and minorities were shut out from learning how to fly, Coleman had traveled to France for flight training and went on to become an excellent, well-respected pilot of her day.

Aerobatics, or "barnstorming," was one of the ways pilots made a living in the pioneering days of aviation. Many barnstorming shows were impromptu affairs, occurring after a pilot buzzed a neighborhood to attract a crowd to a nearby field where he'd land his aircraft. Pilots then performed thrilling feats of aerobatics, such as wing walking, or having a person swing from a trapeze under the fuselage of the airplane. One barnstormer, "Speed" Holeman, became famous for his handkerchief trick, which had him grabbing a handkerchief from a pole while flying upside down. (Holeman later became president of Northwest Airlines.)

After their daring and dangerous stunts, barnstormers passed their leather caps through the crowd for donations, so they could eat and buy more plane fuel. One seasoned barnstormer, when asked what was the most dangerous stunt of barnstorming, answered "starving to death." Many of the greatest pilots of aviation history began their careers as barnstormers.[3]

the postal service to deliver mail in rural areas. They were interested in getting mail delivered to those areas faster, and they looked at the surplus aircraft the government had after World War I. Unfortunately a lot of

Courtesy of Robert F. Zilinsky.

A day at Checkerboard Field in Maywood, Illinois, in the 1920s.

them were de Havilland "Flying Coffins" that had a tendency to catch on fire in flight. Fire was a terrible thing in those days. Plane engines were essentially lubricated with castor oil. Fuel lines weren't what they are today,

and with gasoline being volatile, the planes were highly flammable. You could take one of those old canvas and wood planes, light a match, and in ten minutes the whole plane would be gone. Try doing that today to a Boeing 727.

"The Air Mail Service got going with a bunch of World War I veteran pilots and with war aircraft that weren't designed for air mail. Chicago was the hub. The Air Mail Service is where Chicago really dates its commercial transportation ascendancy because the only way to get air mail from the East Coast to California was through Chicago. The old joke is that pilots used to fly IFR, which we know today as 'Instrument Flight Rules.' In those days it meant 'I fly railroads,' because many pilots used road maps that they'd get from any Texaco station. 'Follow the roads, follow the railroads.'

"They would be up in the air with no navigation aids to speak of, spot a headlight on a Union Pacific or a Pennsylvania train below, and would follow it. And since there were many trains running, they could go from headlight to headlight."

Phil Felper recalls that these pilots "aimed at railroad tracks, rivers, and towns. You get lost and you cry a little, but pretty soon you find out where you are and you think you're pretty brave and smart."

"When commercial air service began to increase, the search was on for another airport. By that time, Cicero Field had closed because the McCormicks had lost interest in aviation and wanted to sell the land. The Aero Club was trying to get Ashburn Field organized, but the airmail service chose a couple of airports in what is Maywood today—Maywood Field and Checkerboard—right across the street from each other. Today, Loyola Hospital is on the site of Maywood Field, and Checkerboard is a forest preserve just south of Roosevelt Road and First Avenue." [DY]

Harold Lind: "Checkerboard didn't become an airmail field until Grant Park was declared too dangerous because of the winds and the flying conditions. Aircraft then were like model airplanes made of balsa wood, and an airport had to be found that would have good flying conditions all year round. Checkerboard was chosen and for two years the air mail came in and went out.

"Earlier, the government was only funding the transcontinental route between New York and San Francisco. The airmail planes would start in New York, fly to Bussletown, Pennsylvania; Bryan, Ohio; and then Chicago's Grant Park, the main stop between here and San Francisco.

Robert Zilinsky's mother on a date at Checkerboard Field in the 1920s. The plane is a JN-4, affectionately known by pilots as a "Jenny."

Courtesy of Robert F. Zilinsky.

Harold Lind is an expert on Chicago's central role in the pioneering days of aviation and the special breed of airmail pilot required to face the dangers of early flying. During his excavations of Checkerboard Field in Maywood—now a forest preserve, but the hub of U.S. airmail flights in 1920—Lind retrieved such artifacts uncovering the old cinder runways as an airspeed indicator from an airmail biplane. Lind spoke of the impact of air mail on Chicago while giving a tour of the green lawns that were once Checkerboard Field.

A monument to the airmail pioneers marks the spot that once was Checkerboard Field in Maywood, Illinois. After Checkerboard Field closed, the Air Mail moved across the street to Maywood Field, on the site of what is today Loyola Hospital.

Trailblazing pilots like Charles Lindbergh flew the mail daily from Maywood Field. It was a dangerous job, but great training for Lindbergh, who later changed the world with his famous 1927 flight from New York to Paris.

Though nearby towns such as Maywood were bustling with aviation activity, Chicago, surprisingly, did not yet have any official airport. There were a few flying fields, but they were privately owned. Once city leaders accepted that aviation was more than a passing fad, a search began to find land for an official municipal airport.

"During its first spring, Checkerboard was hit with a huge snowfall. When the snow melted it soaked the ground and made it very mushy. Many planes landed and nosed over. Airmail service was immediately taken back to Grant Park until cinder runways were installed at Checkerboard, creating a bed planes could safely land on."

Recent exploration of the Checkerboard site has turned up such artifacts as an old brass tag that says "Air Mail Service 89" and an air speed indicator running from 30 to 160 knots that says "U.S. Army."

In his interview, Harold Lind remarked on how many visitors to the park have a hard time visualizing it as an airfield and said that some even doubt that it was ever there. He tells a story about the time he was there searching for evidence of the hangar floors, poking the grass with a long metal probe, and two little kids came racing up and said, "Whatcha doing?" Lind answered, "I'm looking for an airport." One kid turned to the other and said, "An airport? Here? Let's get out of here, this guy's bonkers!"

"When you enter the Checkerboard area from Roosevelt Road, you will find a granite memorial dedicated to the airmail pioneers, intrepid fliers who flew through everything—sleet, storm, lightning, rain, freezing cold—just like their counterparts on foot. Many lost their lives believing in the importance of their mission. Too many scenes were replayed of mothers, wives, and sweethearts waiting at the terminals for them to return from their cross-country flight only to find out they died in a crash on some cornfield." [HL]

Assembly line production of aircraft for the U.S. Air Mail Service.

✈ 1922

The city envisions an Airport Plan that calls for the building of several airports in the Chicago area. One project, endorsed by Mayor William Hale Thompson but later rejected, requires a 10-million dollar landfill in Lake Michigan connected to the mainland by a tunnel near the Field Museum. This plan is obviously the precursor to Meigs Field.[4]

The city's Aeronautical Bureau dedicates a square-mile of land at 63rd Street and Cicero Avenue as an airfield. The field is used primarily for practicing takeoffs and landings by pilots at nearby Maywood and Ashburn Fields.[5]

✈ 1923

A quarter-mile piece of land bordered by Laramie Avenue, Cicero Avenue, and the Belt Railroad tracks at 59th, that Charley Buchmeier once farmed, opens as an air park.[6] The Chicago Air Park Company becomes a tenant on this field and offers flight instructions and aerial photography services.[7]

This same year, the U.S. Post Office begins building 289 signal beacons at 20-mile intervals between Chicago and Cheyenne, Wyoming, for nightly airmail service between Chicago and San Francisco. As part of this ambitious plan, the government rents fields along the route to use as emergency landing sites.[8]

✈ July 1, 1924

The U.S. Post Office begins a New York to San Francisco Air Mail Service, by way of Chicago, for a thirty-day trial. The service proves wildly successful and is continued.[9]

On July 15, the success of the transcontinental airmail route and the continued pressure from pilots and businesses for an all-weather airport spurs Charles H. Wacker, the chairman of the Chicago Plan Commission, to ask the City Council to lease the agricultural land owned by the Board of Education bounded by Cicero Avenue, 55th Street, Central Avenue, and the southern part of 63rd Street for "a Municipal Airplane Landing Field." The Planning Commission recommends the selection because it is ". . . practically the only remaining site of its size, kind, and availability within the City of Chicago."[10]

✈ October 22, 1924

Alderman Dorsey Crowe introduces a resolution requesting that the city's Public Works and Recreation program find a location for an airport for Chicago.[11]

✈ February 2, 1925

President Calvin Coolidge signs into law the Kelly Act, which grants airmail contracts to private companies. Chicago, with its central location, will benefit greatly from such airmail business.[12]

Robertson Aircraft, the company for which Charles Lindbergh flew the mail, is one of several early private commercial charters that come about thanks to Clyde Kelly, representative of Pennsylvania. Kelly authored a bill in Congress turning airmail service over to private carriers. The transportation of mail might have been the short term dream of many private contractors who bid to get into the airmail business, but to Kelly, mail was only a means to an end. Kelly and others were truly visionaries, for they saw air mail as a stepping stone to the eventual birth of commercial aviation. All airlines in the United States can directly trace their birth to 1926 (when the first private contracts were issued) and the Kelly Act.

✈ April 1, 1925

Acting on Alderman Crowe's resolution, City Council approves the ordinance to enter into a 25-year land lease with the Board of Education for six dollars an acre. Soon after, Philip G. Kemp, the Chairman of the Aero Commission, signs a 20-year lease for 300 acres of this land.[13] Kemp constructs a brick and steel hangar and keeps four planes busy with sightseeing tours, charters, and student flying lessons. In photos of the airfield from this year, furrows from farmers plowing the land can be seen.

Kemp's choice of land is a good one for an airport—the airstrip is served by streetcar and it is far enough away from residential areas, leaving pilots extra space to land aircraft in case of emergency.[14]

✈ October 2, 1925

The Post Office awards the first airmail bids to a Chicago airline, National Air Transport (NAT), the precursor to United Airlines.[15] This airline was financed by some of Chicago's most famous citizens, including Marshall Field, William Wrigley, Jr., and Philip D. and Lester Armour.

Courtesy of Robert F. Zilinsky.

The thrilling view from an open cockpit, where a pilot was exposed to the elements.

Pilot Dave Behncke shakes a well-wisher's hand before departing on an airmail run from St. Paul, Minnesota, to Chicago in 1926. Federal Air Mail contracts were the catalyst that would usher in the era of commercial aviation. Behncke, who operated Checkerboard Field in Maywood, went on to found the Airline Pilots Association.

Mail being loaded into a National Air Transport (NAT) plane. NAT, after consolidation with other airlines, became United Air Lines.

New hangars are built to house aircraft for National Air Transport at Chicago Municipal Airport, late 1920s.

"People didn't understand that airmail pilots were doing some of the toughest flying in the world. The most hazardous was in the Midwest where the weather is notoriously bad, especially in wintertime, when a schedule had to be met while flying in planes not equipped for ice and snow and fog." [TG]

The experiences of one airmail pilot nicknamed "Slim" are legendary. His job was flying mail for Robertson Aircraft, which won a contract for a particular route centering on Chicago from the U.S. Post Office, which had ascertained it was cheaper to farm out the service. On the night of September 16, 1926, Slim took off from Peoria, and as his DH-4 rose above the airport, he realized the weather was dangerous and would undoubtedly get worse along his route. His first impulse was to drop a flare to guide him back to the landing strip. When he hit the flare button, however, nothing happened. He decided to push ahead through the fog to Chicago, where he might find a hole in the clouds to make a safe landing.

Over Maywood, he still couldn't find an opening. He turned west, trying to spot one of the beacons he knew was along the transcontinental route. Not a flicker; the weather continued to block his vision.

Minutes later, Slim's engine started to cough and sputter, which meant his main fuel tank was running dry. He quickly activated the auxiliary tank. But even though the engine began to run

Top to bottom: Logos of National Air Transport (1928), Northwest Airlines (1934), and American Airlines (1932). In the 1920s, Robertson Aircraft, which flew the mail from St. Louis to the Chicago area, evolved into American Airlines.

properly again, Slim knew his luck would soon run out.

Suddenly, through the cloud canopy below, he saw a faint glow. Hoping it was the lights of a town, he activated his flare release again, and this time it worked.

As the flare dropped, glowing red through the mist, Slim calculated that it would be only a matter of time until he completely ran out of fuel. The flare disappeared quickly, swallowed by the mist.

With his auxiliary tank just about empty, Slim pulled back on the stick and let his de Havilland shoot up into the moonlight. He climbed higher, remembering pilot talk about how altitude was like money in the bank—one could always draw from it. He must have felt very much alone in that cockpit, 5,000 feet above earth, his view shrouded by an impenetrable white canopy.

Then, as he knew it would, the engine sputtered and died. He was out of fuel. He slipped off the belt that held him in the cockpit, threw himself over the side, and pulled the ripcord of his parachute. Through the darkness, as he floated down, he heard a sound that surprised him. It was the drone of an active airplane engine—his airplane engine.

It dawned on Slim what had happened. As he was climbing, desperately trying to gain altitude, the angle had pulled the little remaining fuel away from the engine. After he bailed out, the plane had leveled, and the fuel returned to its proper place.

As Slim dangled under his parachute, he must have felt his chances were slim as he watched his plane circle and fly straight towards him. He saw his luck return as the speeding plane missed him by 100 yards before spiraling downward.

Then, as if in a Buster Keaton silent movie, the plane turned again and made a second pass at Slim. Again the plane missed him. Before it finally crashed, it made four more passes, closely missing the pilot each time. He floated to a safe landing on the outskirts of Ottawa, Illinois, a sleepy farm town, and began walking.

Along a stretch of lonely road, the headlights of a car driven by 17-year-old Julio Corsini caught the bedraggled figure of a man in a leather flight suit. Corsini was working that night at the local air strip, the same one that Slim was trying to find. A phone call from Chicago had alerted Corsini that there was a plane somewhere in the area trapped by the weather, and the pilot would attempt to fly to Ot-tawa. Corsini was listening intently for a plane engine, and when he heard it he lit several 50-gallon drums of fuel, hoping the flames could be seen by the pilot through the cloud cover. Slim flew his DH-4 over the airport, but because of the fog never saw it.

Corsini picked Slim up, drove into Ottawa, and the two of them sat in a diner for the rest of the night, drinking coffee and talking about flying.

Corsini didn't think much more about the tall stranger he picked up on the road that night in September, until eight months later, when he read about how that same pilot, "Slim" Charles Lindbergh, flew across the Atlantic non-stop from New York to Paris and changed the world.

Lindbergh couldn't ask for better training for his record flight than being alone in an old biplane that wasn't designed to fly in snow and sleet, humping the mail between St. Louis and Chicago through terrible weather in an unreliable aircraft. And yet, amid all the dangers, it was no wonder that Lucky Lindy flew the mail, for he wrote years later that "to be a pilot of the night mail appeared the summit of ambition for a flier."[16]

"No one could fly the air mail except pilots who were pretty tough and would fly in impossible weather. There weren't too many around. Lindbergh and the others would come into the old terminal and climb into the open cockpits; the mail would be brought in by cars and trucks, thrown up to the pilots, and away they'd go. Later on, the short hauls would include Detroit; South Bend, Indiana; and places like that.

Charles A. Lindbergh flew the mail for Robertson Aircraft, 1926.

Children on a tour of the National Air Transport facilities at Chicago Municipal, late 1920s.

"Flying west was tougher because of the mountainous territory. The airplanes didn't have the best engines in the world, so many times the pilots had to make forced landings in fields." [PF]

"The Pony Express in the 1800s was considered a big step for progress—moving information quickly from one point to another. It lasted only eight months, rendered obsolete by the invention of the telegraph.

"Checkerboard Field suffered the same fate, having become obsolete after a year to eighteen months because it was too small to accommodate the planes that were getting bigger and bigger by the day." [HL]

"The next big step in delivering mail by air was the privatizing of the service, accomplished in 1926 by the Kelly Air Mail Act. The federal government wanted to get out of the business of running an airline; under the act they were able to contract AirMail Service to anyone with an airplane. All commercial airlines in the United States date their history from the act.

"As a result of the Kelly Act, two important events occurred that impacted on Chicago's role in the aviation industry. One was the assembling of a group of entrepreneurs in Chicago to put together what eventually became United Air Lines. Pop Dickenson also tried to start up another airline between Chicago and Minneapolis that proved to be a failure. He hired some good pilots but didn't have the capital to keep it going so he was

From the Lynch family collection.

Municipal Airport in 1926 when it was still very much a farmer's field, rather than an airport with paved runways. Cicero Avenue is on the bottom of the photo, and the Chicago and Western Indiana Railroad track cuts west to east to the left in the photo.

A schedule from 1929, which includes all of the daily flights in the United States, lists one flight from New York to Chicago, of several hours, with a caption stating that the passenger may have to share the ride with a sack of mail. Airlines like United Air Lines, Chicago and Southern, and Northwest Airlines did not necessarily want to cater to passengers when mail proved to be even more profitable.

bought out.

"The second event was that the act spurred Chicago into realizing that if it were going to be a major player in the aviation game, it was going to have to build a first-class airport. A first-class airport in those days consisted of a couple of 2,000-feet gravel runways, a clear zone, and some sort of a building in which passengers could wait for their planes. Even though aviation activity was bustling at nearby towns like Maywood, Chicago, surprisingly, did not yet have any official airport. There were a few flying fields, but they were privately owned. With city leaders accepting that aviation was more than a passing fad, a search began to find land for an official municipal airport.

"There had been a flying field on the South Side earlier, in the area that is now Midway Airport. The Chicago Board of Education owned the land under a nineteenth century land grant. The city made a quick deal with the Board giving them use of the land, and they managed to organize an airport called Chicago Municipal Airport. If they hadn't, Chicago's principal airport at the time would have gone to the suburbs." [DY]

✈

1. David M. Young and Neal Callahan, *Fill the Heavens with Commerce: Chicago Aviation, 1855–1926* (Chicago: Chicago Review Press, 1981), 118.

2. Robert M. Hill, *A Little Known Story of the Land Called Clearing* (Chicago: Chicago Historical Society, 1983), 168.

3. Ibid., 168, 198.

4. Young, 149.

5. Ibid.

6. Hill, 168.

7. Young, 149.

8. Ibid.

9. Ibid.

10. Ibid., 150.

11. Ibid.

12. Ibid.

13. Ibid.

14. Hill, 172.

15. Young, 151.

16. Donald Dale Jackson, *Flying the Mail.* Epic of Flight (Alexandria, Virginia: Time-Life Books, 1982), 148.

Part II

From Municipal Airport to Midway Airport
1926–1945

✈

Fledgling airlines based out of Chicago Municipal in 1928. Left to right: The first three hangars were owned by National Air Transport, Boeing Air Transport had the next two, and the 108th Air National Guard Observation Squadron was based out of the hangar with the beacon above. National Air Transport and Boeing Air Transport eventually merged and became United Air Lines.

✈ From Onion Field to Airport

✈ **May 8th, 1926**

Chicago's Municipal Airport is officially unveiled, "with a great deal of hoopla but very little business." Pilot Edmund Marucha flew a $30,000 Curtiss Carrier Pigeon, owned by National Air Transport and renamed *Miss Chicago*, from Maywood Field to Municipal. Four carrier pigeons are released with messages for officials in Washington. Alderman Crowe, in a speech at the opening, anticipates that Chicago's newest airport would have a major impact on the city's business.[1]

Canvas hangars are built on Cicero Avenue. According to one eyewitness, whenever a strong gust of wind came along, the canvas hangars were blown over.[2]

❝The airmail connection had moved across the street from Checkerboard to Maywood Airfield. Then, in 1927, the federal government announced they were going to transfer the air mail from Maywood to Municipal Airport (now Midway) in Chicago, and from there it would be farmed out to the many private airlines," relates Harold Lind.

Municipal was located on a one-mile-square onion field with a grammar school on the southwest end. The land belonged to the Chicago Board of Education through an eighty-year-old land grant program under which the federal government dedicated one mile in every 365 for a school. Midway Airport remains on that one-square-mile plot.

When Municipal opened, it was primarily a field for private aviators. There was some commercial airline activity, but it was relatively minor. Within a few years, however, the airport began to hum.

The first commercial airplane landed at Chicago's newly-dedicated Municipal Airport from Omaha, Nebraska, on December 1, 1927—a Boeing commercial aircraft piloted by Ira Biffle. Only six months earlier on May 30, 1927, fellow airmail pilot Charles Lindbergh had moved on from flying the mail from St. Louis to Chicago and into the history books. No doubt Biffle was pleased, for not only was Lucky Lindy a member of the club, but Biffle had also taught Lindy to fly.

Lindbergh planned his transatlantic attempt carefully. As Felper describes it, "every spare spot on *The Spirit of St. Louis* carried fuel, including the windshields, so he had only a small periscope for forward vision. Otherwise, he looked out of the side windows.

"The highest he could fly was ten thousand feet. He stayed three or four thousand feet above the water, which meant if any storms occurred he was in dire trouble. He had no weather broadcasts; he flew in the general direction of Ireland, which was difficult because he had nothing to home in on. He fell asleep several times and would wake up just before dunking

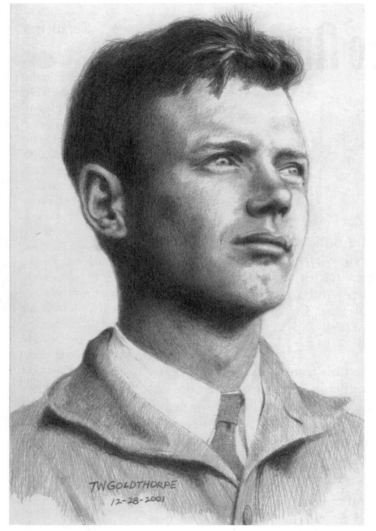

Drawing by Thomas W. Goldthorpe.

Charles A. Lindbergh.

From the Lynch family collection.

A replica of the *Sprit of St. Louis* parked at Midway Airport in 1977, the fiftieth anniversary of Lindbergh's famous flight across the Atlantic.

✈ May 30, 1927

Charles Lindbergh, piloting the *Spirit of St. Louis*, flies from New York to Paris, in the first transatlantic solo flight, in 33 hours, 29 minutes, 30 seconds.

✈ August 13, 1927

Thousands gather in Soldier Field to salute Lindbergh when the "Lone Eagle" lands his *Spirit of St. Louis* in Chicago.

Photo by the Chicago Daily News. Courtesy of the Chicago Historical Society (glass negative: DN-0084173).

Charles Lindbergh arrives in the *Spirit of St. Louis* at Chicago Municipal Airport
on August 13, 1927, and is given a police motorcycle escort off the field.

The path of planes' wheels can be seen running through the pasture on the left, c. 1928. In the center, a figure in white is turning the biplane's propeller. Hand-propping, as it was called, was extremely dangerous, and pilots were sometimes killed attempting the maneuver. The hangar in the background was run by Aviation Service and Transport School of Aviation, which went out business during the Depression. The space would become Monarch Air Service's first hangar.

From the Lynch family collection.

✈ July 1, 1927

The U.S. Army bases its 108th Squadron 33rd Division Illinois Air National Guard at Municipal. A senior instructor by the name of George Marshall is assigned to the 108th between 1933 and 1936. Marshall will go on to to become President Franklin Roosevelt's Chief of Staff, and later, as President Truman's Secretary of State, the architect of "The Marshall Plan," which helped feed Europe after the destruction of World War II.[3]

Two cinder runways, 1200 and 1500 feet long (and 90 feet wide), are constructed, and the City Council awards $10,000 for maintenance and salaries for personnel to oversee the airfield. The Department of Public Works takes administrative control of the area through its Bureau of Parks, Recreation and Aviation and is held responsible for the field's maintenance and control.[4]

2,367 passengers take off from Municipal Airport in airplanes owned or operated by flying clubs and sightseeing companies, compared with only 34 passengers carried by a scheduled airline.[5]

✈ December 1927

The first airmail flight arrives at Chicago Municipal Airport from Omaha, Nebraska on the first of the month. The flight is piloted by Ira O. Biffle who flies for Boeing Air Transport, the forerunner of United Air Lines.

On the 12th, Mayor William H. Thompson officially re-dedicates the property as Chicago Municipal Airport—just six months after Lindbergh's historic flight across the Atlantic. By the end of the year, 800 flights take off and land at Municipal.[6] Six airlines operate from Municipal, including the predecessors of Braniff, Northwest, Eastern, TWA, Chicago and Southern, and United. Pacific Air Transport would merge with National Air Transport, Boeing Air Transport, and Varney Airlines to form United Air Lines.[7]

Chicago Municipal Airport in 1928, with the National Air Transport (NAT) hangar in the background.

✈ 1928

The fleet of airplanes at Municipal reaches 100. The field has twelve more hangars; more runways, taxiways, and ramps; and up-to-date field lighting for night landings.[8] By year's end, there are 41,660 flights and 15,498 passengers. Note that flights outnumber passengers over 2 to 1. One reason is that most flights are used to fly the mail.[9]

✈ 1929

Air traffic control comes to the airport in the form of the "flagman" who stations himself at the takeoff end of the runway. The flagman moves around the field as the wind dictates and gives the "all clear" signal to the pilot when it is safe for takeoff. Due to the crowds of people that continue to show up and watch airplanes land and take off, the city assigns police to keep the crowds at bay.

Charles Downey, the youngest naval aviator of World War II, has an impressive aviation résumé, ranging from being awarded the Distinguished Flying Cross for assisting in sinking a Japanese cruiser with his Hellfighter in Manila Harbor in 1944, to being one of the early executives that brought Midway Airlines to prominence in the 1980s. Based at Midway Airport with American Airlines from 1952 through to their eventual relocation to O'Hare, Downey's observations on the challenge of Midway Airport to weather those dark days in its history add much to the story of the airport.

into the ocean. Years later, I flew the Atlantic in a DC-4, and it was tough on me! In his much smaller plane with a lot less power and no electronic gear it was near impossible."

"Shortly before Lindbergh's flight, two French World War I heroes, Charles Nungesser and Francois Coli, tried making the flight from Paris to New York. No trace of them was ever found. Lindbergh alluded to their valiant effort when he reached Paris, and the French were very grateful." [TG]

"What drove Lindbergh, besides the prize money," explains Charles Downey, "was the fact that if the plane could be depended on, if you put enough fuel in it and it stayed in one piece, it could fly anywhere." Goldthorpe adds, "the Wrights invented the airplane; Lindbergh demonstrated its potential."

Some time after his historic flight, Lindbergh visited Chicago's newest airport in the *Spirit of St. Louis*. As he taxied his famous plane off the runway, he received an escort from a phalanx of policemen on motorcycles. People came out by the thousands to greet him.

Today, flight passengers frequently complain about the food on short flights, often just a bag of peanuts. In the early days of commercial aviation, passengers received no food and had to sit on mailbags. The planes were really designed for one person—the pilot—and a little space for baggage, principally mail. All the private flight schedules of airlines in the United States in 1929 could fit on a letter-size sheet of paper. Charles Downey showed the author one such schedule that contained the note: "One passen-

ger transported daily in an open mail plane, subject to weather conditions and loading. Additional passenger service to be provided soon."

"What made Municipal Airport important was the same thing that made Chicago the railroad center and a center of highways—it was located in the middle of the country. In those days planes couldn't fly very far, so they had to travel in hops, and Chicago was a main hop stop." [DY]

Chicago still a railroad hub in those days, pilots could watch trains as they made their final approach into Chicago Municipal and use the tracks to orient themselves. Bordering the field was the railroad track of the heaviest traveled line in the United States, with deep ruts on either side. Pilots had to be very careful with their takeoffs and landings because the one runway that avoided the ruts was too short.

By the end of 1927, the new airport saw eight hundred airplanes take off and land. By 1928, that number exploded to over forty-one thousand planes having carried over fifteen thousand passengers. By the end of the 1920s, Municipal had become the busiest airport in the world—a title it would hold until the 1960s.

Aviation was changing and so too was America. As air travel fought for respectability, immigrants from Europe continued to settle in the large cities looking for the American Dream. One of the new arrivals from Ireland was Pierce O'Carroll, nicknamed Scotty (the author's grandfather), whose only dream was to fly.

✈ **1930**

After negotiating for two years, the City of Chicago leases a portion of a square-mile plot of land for aviation use. In November, the City Council passes a bond issue of $450,000 to be used for the construction of more runways, taxiways, sewers, and ramp space. An east-west runway is increased in length from 2,400 feet to 4,900 feet. The lengthening of the runways is in response to new, larger aircraft, such as the Tri-motor that can seat 14 persons, as well as accommodate mail.

Commercial flights are so numerous that student lessons are discouraged, though unsuccessfully.[10]

From the Lynch family collection.

A view of Chicago Municipal, facing south, with the Belt Railway tracks running on the north side of the field, late 1930s.

From the Lynch family collection.

Left: Pilot Pierce "Scotty" O'Carroll in 1932, founder of Monarch Air Service, an aviation business headquartered at Chicago Municipal Airport. O'Carroll began as a barnstormer and over the next three decades would have a strong influence at the airport.

Below, left: A Fleet biplane trainer owned by Monarch Air Service.

Below, right: A Travelaire E-4000 primary trainer, owned and operated by Monarch Air Service in the early 1930s at Chicago Municipal Airport. Notice in the background the train traveling along the Belt Railway tracks that bordered the north end of the airfield. A student pilot later crashed this plane onto those tracks.

Summer was the best time to make money from renting or chartering aircraft. But when the snow began to fly in November, Scotty O'Carroll took a crew of people barnstorming to the warmer South. They would fly over a town—with one of the airplanes trailing smoke to get attention—and the airplanes would be met at the local airstrip or nearby field by a curious crowd. Then, O'Carroll and his crew would hustle for fares.

Left: A Beech D18-A parked in front of Monarch Air Service, 1930s. (Courtesy of Robert F. Zilinsky.)

Above: A young Pierce O'Carroll, right, poses in front of an airplane, 1920s. (From the Lynch family collection.)

"Scotty is one of Midway's legends. He goes way back in its early history, working fourteen to sixteen hours a day—promoting aviation, doing charters, doing anything he could to bring aviation into the foreground." [CD]

Phil Felper, who knew O'Carroll well, describes Scotty as "a big Irishman with a brogue so thick you could cut it. And sharp. A very good, hardworking man."

O'Carroll was a member of a large family from Gregavalla in County Leix, Ireland. Wanting to make his fortune, the ambitious Scotty went into steeplechase racing and was winning serious prize money. His father, with the responsibility of supporting the big family, routinely borrowed a portion of the winnings. He never repaid Scotty.

Not satisfied with horse racing, the adventurous young Irishman saw a few very old, early airplanes flying overhead and fell in love with the idea of becoming a pilot. Ireland held little chance of this, so he emigrated to the United States, to Chicago, in 1924 to pursue the adventure of aviation.

His daughter Sheila remembers that he drove buses at first to make a living, but wanted to fly so badly that he took his first lesson in a JN-4 "Jenny" at the now-defunct Ashburn Field at 83rd Street and Cicero Avenue.

O'Carroll enjoyed the sensation of flying so much, he made arrangements to have another lesson the day after his first one. When he arrived for his second lesson, the instructor was not yet there. Being a bit of

Sheila O'Carroll Lynch.
As a young woman, Sheila flew with her father Pierce "Scotty" O'Carroll, one of the early pilots to fly out of Municipal Airport. He would eventually start Monarch Air Service there.

Courtesy of Robert F. Soraparu.

An American Airways Stinson Reliant parked at Chicago Municipal Airport. The four-passenger Reliant was used for route surveys, as well as for training, beginning in 1933.

a daredevil, O'Carroll decided to take the plane up anyway.

As the instructor arrived as Ashburn Field, he could see the JN-4 aircraft sailing overhead, with O'Carroll at the controls. When O'Carroll finally brought the plane down for a landing, the instructor silently strolled up to O'Carroll, looked him in the eye, and said, "Pierce . . . you passed." Although he may not have known it at the time, O'Carroll had

Fred Farbin. It was a ride on a Ferris Wheel in 1944 that would change Fred Farbin's life. Fred and a friend found themselves temporarily stopped on top of a Ferris Wheel at a carnival at 63rd and Cicero. As they waited, Fred watched the planes landing at nearby Chicago Municipal Airport and suggested to his friend that they go over and check out the airplanes. The two teenagers crossed the street and saw a sign advertising Monarch sightseeing flights. After buying their tickets, Fred climbed into the cockpit of a Stinson SR-9. The pilot, Pierce "Scotty" O'Carroll, chatted with him a bit and soon asked Fred if he wanted a job. Fred said *yes*, and except for a tour in the Merchant Marines during World War II, Monarch Air Service was his life's work over the next four decades. In 1985, shortly before Farbin's death, the author sat down with him to record an interview about Midway's past. Farbin's comments have been transcribed from that interview.

finally found his calling, a profession he would practice for the next forty years.

Sheila Lynch: "It was the time of the Depression. During the week Scotty worked for the bus company by day and went to school at night. On weekends he flew solo and gave lessons." O'Carroll continued driving the bus and flying in his free time, until a disagreement about his bus uniform helped to decide his future.

Fred Farbin, who worked for Scotty, recalled: "He got a job driving a bus for Chicago Motor Coach on Michigan Avenue. Of course he was his own man, and he was always being reprimanded for not wearing his cap while he was driving the bus. Then one day his boss pulled him over and told him, 'Either put the cap on, or get off the bus,' . . . so he got off the bus!"

"Above all else, he yearned to have his own flying business, so he decided to start Monarch Air Service, which proved to be the longest, continuously managed fix-based aviation company in United States aviation history." [SL]

✈

1. David M. Young and Neal Callahan, *Fill the Heavens with Commerce: Chicago Aviation, 1855–1926* (Chicago: Chicago Review Press, 1981), 151–2.

2. Robert M. Hill, *A Little Known Story of the Land Called Clearing* (Chicago: Chicago Historical Society, 1983), 172.

3. Ibid., 211.

4. John A. Casey, *Forty Years of Chicago Aviation: 1926–1966* (Chicago Department of Aviation, 1966), 1.

5. Ibid., 3.

6. Hill, 173.

7. Ibid.

8. Casey, 3.

9. Hill, 173.

10. Casey, 5.

11. Neil Steinberg, "Doomed Flight Had a Strong Tie With Chicago," *Chicago Sun-Times*, 8 March 2001.

Mike Rezich, who lived his entire life across the street from Midway Airport, recalled the days when the airport was surrounded by prairie. His older brother, a pilot, often landed at Chicago Municipal and, because there was no fence, taxied the airplane down the street to the family's house and parked it in the backyard.

From the Lynch family collection.

An attendant checks passengers' tickets before they board an American Airways Pilgrim at Chicago Municipal, early 1930s.

Courtesy of the City of Chicago, Department of Aviation.

Passengers board an early airplane on the left while mail is loaded onto the plane from the right. Air travel in the late 1920s had few perks, with passengers often sharing space with mail bags. For the airlines in those days, flying the mail was more lucrative than flying passengers.

✈ The Lituanica

In Marquette Park, at the corner of California and Marquette Avenues, stands a majestic winged granite statue commemorating a long forgotten transatlantic flight that still remains important to Chicago's Lithuanian community. If there is any doubt about this, ask any Chicagoan of Lithuanian descent, and they will recite for you the story of Stephen Darius and Stanley Girenas.

In 1933, it had been six years since Charles A. Lindbergh crossed the Atlantic in the *Spirit of St. Louis.* Lindbergh, however, had flown to Paris. Darius and Girenas wanted to fly to Lithuania. To raise the funds to do so, a pledge of two dollars got a donor a ride in *The Lituanica,* a Bellanca CH-300 Pacemaker, and one's name listed on the fabric of the monoplane. The plane was based at Chicago Municipal Airport in a hangar at 5240 W. 63rd St.

Darius and Girenas took off from New York for the 4,400-mile flight to Kaunas, Lithuania. They never made it. Bad weather may have been the factor for their crash in Germany, 400 miles short of their target. Their legacy abides not only in the monument in Marquette Park but in the street in the Bridgeport neighborhood named Lituanica for their aircraft.[11]

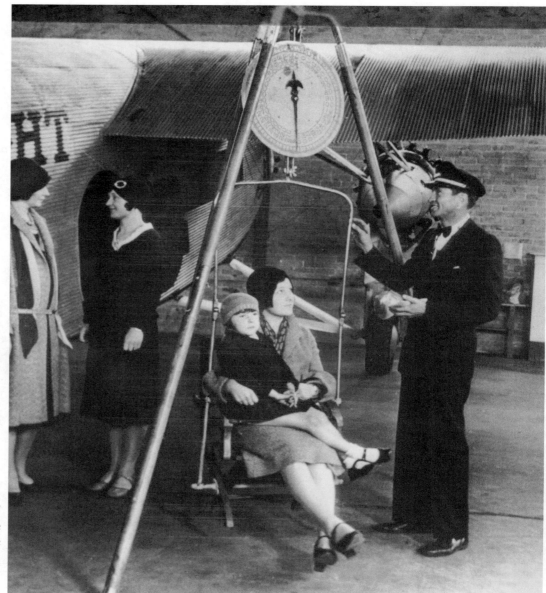

A mother and her child "weigh in" before departure, early 1930s. Aircraft like the Tri-motor behind them could only handle certain weight loads in order to fly safely.

Courtesy of the City of Chicago, Department of Aviation.

The planes may have been primitive in the early days of commercial aviation, but the service could be elegant.

Passengers board a United Air Lines Boeing 80-A aircraft at Chicago Municipal Airport, 1930s.

The Tri-Motor and the DC-3

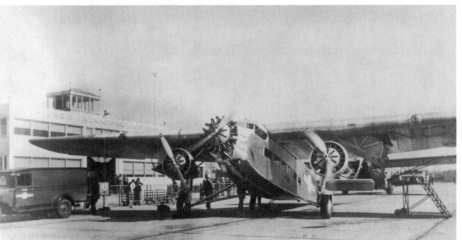

After Municipal Airport began operating, development of commercially feasible aircraft—planes large enough to carry goods *and* passengers and to make money at it—was badly needed.

Phil Felper remembers: "The early airlines had very slow, usually fabric, planes with no radios. All flying was done visually with no directional instruments. They had Curtiss Condors, very large two-engine planes made of fabric, and Stinson Tri-motors, with either high or low wings. And that was it. These planes carried no more than eight to ten passengers."

The later Ford Tri-motor was the first moderately successful commercial aircraft. It was an improvement on the Curtiss and the Stinson, but its small size, slow speed, and limited passenger capacity would hinder commercial aviation until a still bigger and more powerful plane could be built. Nevertheless, all the airlines at that time used it.

"In 1931, a Dutchman named Fokker, who had built many of the World War I German fighter planes, introduced a wooden tri-motor commercial plane that was slow and durable and carried a maximum of twelve passengers or a like amount of freight. Then, in 1931, famed Notre Dame football coach Knute Rockne died in a Fokker crash while flying to California from South Bend, Indiana. The wing had dropped off and the plane fell apart over Bizarre,

A Boeing Air Transport (United) Tri-motor parked in front of the terminal at Chicago Municipal Airport, early 1930s.

Courtesy of Robert F. Soraparu.

A Tri-motor takes on mail. Even though commercial airlines were flying passengers frequently in the early 1930s, the airlines continued to get most of their revenue from flying the mail for the Post Office.

A United Air Lines Tri-motor in front of the terminal at Chicago Municipal, early 1930s.

Several airplanes lined up in front of the terminal building at Chicago Municipal, early 1930s. Since there was only one gate—through the chain-link fence in front of the terminal—aircraft would line up as in a taxi queue and pull into position to load passengers.

Crowds of people visited Midway Airport to stand against the fence and watch celebrities fly in—typically between 4 P.M. and 6 P.M. according to one old-timer. In the early 1930s, the aircraft the airlines operated, Curtiss Condors, Boeing 80-As, Lockheed Vegas, or Tri-motors, only carried a few passengers. The Boeing 247 held twelve passengers, as did the Lockheed Electra, which had a cruising speed of 150 MPH.

Courtesy of the City of Chicago, Department of Aviation.

Hundreds of people gather to look at airplanes at Chicago Municipal Airport, early 1930s. Airplanes were still a novelty, and crowds would often gather to see the arrival of movie stars on the commercial carriers.

Kansas. The country was stunned and the federal government raced in, grounded the Fokkers, and conducted the first federal investigation of an aviation disaster. This gave the Ford Tri-motor a great competitive advantage.

"Fokker was never able to recover; the wooden airplane was doomed for commercial service; and the well-reported tragedy had a dampening effect on the public's desire to use flying as transportation." [DY]

Young also suggests that the broad fear of flying was dramatically reversed during the 1932 Democratic presidential convention in Chicago. New York governor Franklin Delano Roosevelt was favored to be the party's choice. A fledgling enterprise called

American Airlines convinced him that if he were nominated he should fly to Chicago to make his acceptance speech.

"FDR thought it was a fine idea. American had a Ford Tri-motor waiting in Albany, and when the good news was announced, the governor flew to Chicago, making several stops on the way for press conferences.

"The flight received worldwide publicity, culminating in the historic photo of FDR deplaning at Chicago Municipal Airport, waving, and wearing his famous toothy smile for the hordes of news reporters and photographers. This scene of the future President of the United States flying in an airplane served to allay the public's fear of flying.

"The Douglas DC-3, which succeeded the Ford Tri-motor, was a quantum leap in commercial aircraft. Boeing had built the 247 earlier; it was better than the Tri-motor, but was outperformed in every way by the DC-3. Douglas built thousands of these ships, some of which are still in use today. They became the dominant aircraft and were put to commercial use as fast as Douglas could turn them out. It remained aviation's workhorse well into World War II." [DY]

Even the DC-3, a plane that pilots loved to fly, had its own unique hazards in the air. Phil Felper, a pilot whose career began with American Airlines in 1939 and progressed to the flying of corporate jets in the 1980s, recalls: "The run from Chicago to New York in a DC-3 took four hours. Many times you were in the middle of a thunderstorm before you

Three DC-3s lined up in front of the old terminal at Chicago Municipal Airport, late 1930s. The DC-3 made it profitabile for the airlines to fly passengers.

Courtesy of the City of Chicago, Department of Aviation.

Photo by the Chicago Daily News. Courtesy of the Chicago Historical Society (glass negative: DN-0100254).

Democratic Presidential nominee Franklin D. Roosevelt breaks with tradition and flies to Chicago to accept his party's nomination. He is seen here with his son James (left) on the tarmac of Chicago Municipal Airport as a large crowd presses up towards him and the Ford Tri-motor that flew him from Albany, New York.

To appreciate how radically FDR's in-person acceptance of his party's nomination bucked tradition, one has only to study nineteenth-century political convention history.

✈

When the Republican Convention met in Chicago in 1860, candidate Abraham Lincoln passed the time in Springfield playing a variation of handball in a vacant lot next to the *Illinois State Journal* office, waiting for a telegram of news from the convention floor. The day after the party's decision, May 19, a delegation traveled to Springfield to formally present the nomination to Lincoln.

✈

The meeting did not begin well as the Lincolns had just had an argument on whether alcohol should be served to their guests. Matters were made even more uncomfortable when several of the traveling delegates who had never seen Lincoln in person were startled by his rough-hewn appearance.[2]

The interior of Chicago Municipal Airport's terminal, built 1931.

Courtesy of Robert F. Soraparu.

An American Airlines DC-2, *Flagship Dallas*, at Chicago Municipal Airport. It was American Airlines' first DC-2 and placed into service between Chicago and Newark on December 1, 1934.

✈ **1933**

As part of the "Century of Progress" World's Fair, an air show is held on the southern end of Municipal Field. People come from throughout Chicago to watch parachute jumpers and aerobatics, such as a Ford Tri-motor attempt an inside loop.[3]

In addition to the air show, the World's Fair hosts the International Air Race, an exhibition of exhilarating speed and endurance. Racers in their specially designed aircraft speed between two giant pylons—one at Municipal Field, the other at Hawthorne Race Track—banking their aircraft at 90 degree turns, their wings barely missing the ground.[4]

Before he became famous to the rest of the world with his daring air raids over Tokyo during World War II, air racer Jimmy Doolittle visits Chicago Municipal, along with other racing aces, like Roscoe Turner, an extravagant pilot that used to fly with a pet lion. In the 1930s, air racers were as popular as movie stars.

A radio control tower is established at the field, allowing two-way radio communication between the tower and the pilot.[5]

Courtesy of Robert F. Zilinsky.

A Pennsylvania Central DC-3A parked at Chicago Municipal. Pennsylvania Central began service from Chicago in 1939, but would stop service by 1950.

From the Lynch family collection.

The Chicago Municipal Airport terminal with DC-3s lined up on the tarmac, late 1930s. Note the small parking lot behind the terminal. The American Airlines hangar can be seen on the top right.

knew it, because unless there was daylight and you could visually see the build-up ahead, you had no way of knowing in advance. Then you'd try to avoid it one way or another. If you couldn't, the rain would come right through the windshield—so much rain that we'd get the stewardesses to put raincoats on us backwards to keep our clothes dry. You took your shoes off to keep water from piling up and soaking your feet.

"Flocks of birds could also be a lethal threat. During migrating season, for instance, when a flock of geese hit your plane, they could take the windshield out and kill the pilot. To combat this, a stainless steel post called a 'duck post' would be built down the windshield's center and would cut the goose in half when it hit. Windows in the rest of the plane could not be protected, so during migration the pilot had to be very careful. The birds made one hell of a bang.

"You also had mechanical problems. If you lost an engine shortly after takeoff, you'd have enough time to get back to the field. If not, you sweated a bit, looked for another spot to land, such as a baseball field, a park, anything open. You'd also do a lot of praying on the way down! Pilots in those early days of unreliable engines were often forced down in emer-

Above: Airplanes, many of which were made of fabric, could be easily damaged from a collision with a bird, as evidenced by this aircraft's wing.
Left: A Stinson Tri-motor NC-11153, owned by Monarch Air Service and used for sightseeing, late 1930s.

From the Lynch family collection.

gencies more times than they cared for.

"I remember how Scotty O'Carroll used to handle such situations. He'd carry passengers just to give them a ride, $3.50 a ride. And he'd lose engines, sometimes over the lakefront, sometimes over Grant Park. In Chicago in those days there were many designated strips to land on in an emergency situa-

tion. We now have expressways on many of those very places."

One of the designated spots was the Soldier Field parking lot. O'Carroll once made an emergency landing in the parking lot. A crowd gathered to see him, his tool kit by his side, as he repaired an engine. Someone asked him how he was going to get the

Aviation was still such a novelty in the 1930s that sightseeing over the city remained popular. The old terminal was where the sightseeing planes were kept, chocked up on the tarmac side of the field, with a cyclone fence separating the parking lot from the airfield. Competition for customers was vicious, and one reason was because of the $2 fare—a generous payment during the lean years of the Great Depression that could be commanded because of the 1933 World's Fair.

"Scotty" O'Carroll stationed his flying tours north of the terminal, while his competition was to the south, including George Baker, who also kept two Ryan aircraft there. Baker went on to found National Airlines in Florida.

✈

Right: A Stinson Tri-motor NC-11153, flown by Pierce "Scotty" O'Carroll over Chicago's lakefront, late 1930s. Sightseeing was a big part of O'Carroll's early business. Grant Park and the Illinois Central Railroad can be seen below.

From the Lynch family collection.

5 unharmed as plane lands on lake front

Four passengers aboard a sight-seeing plane got an unexpected thrill Sunday when their pilot made an emergency "dead stick" landing on a narrow strip at 36th St. and Lake Shore Dr.

The pilot, Zenon Skar, 31, of 4980 N. Major Ave., was making a tour over the city when the plane ran out of gas at an altitude of 2,200 feet.

Skar, an ex-Army pilot, had made the sight-seeing run scores of times and had worked out a series of landing spots for such emergencies.

"I picked one where there was no traffic and dropped the plane in," he said.

He made a perfect landing on a strip 75 yards wide and 175 yards long. No one was injured.

The plane, a single-engine Stinson, is owned by Monarch Air Service Inc. at Municipal Airport.

Passengers aboard the plane were Mrs. William Joyce, of 1005 E. Marquette Rd., her small child, and a Mr. and Mrs. Zomek, of East Chicago, Ind.

plane out of the lot. O'Carroll said he was going to bring it out the same way he brought it in, by flying it out, even though the path was short and marred by trees. He fired up the engine, and after a wave to the crowd, his airplane roared into the air, just clearing the trees.

"That's Scotty. That's why everybody really went for him. There was nothing that Scotty wouldn't do. he'd say, 'if anybody can do it, I can do it.' Same with flying. He'd say, 'if the birds can fly, I can fly.' But I'll tell you, a guy like him drove you." [PF]

Ironically, a few years later, another pilot for Monarch would land a Stinson Reliant SR-9 in the south parking lot of Soldier Field. Monarch's loyal employee Fred Farbin drove to the lakefront and slept in the airplane so that parts wouldn't be stolen from it, and the next day he replaced the broken cylinder that had forced the plane down. Scotty O'Carroll came back down to Soldier Field to again fly one of his planes out of its parking lot.

"It's a funny thing," Fred remembered four decades later, "the people on that ride came back and wanted half their money back, since they didn't get the full ride."

Takes Off from Soldiers' Field Lot

SOLDIERS' FIELD

PARKING LOT

Sightseeing plane flying from parking lot south of Soldiers' field yesterday after forced landing there on Sunday. [TRIBUNE Photo.]

From the Lynch family collection.

Left: A newspaper report about a forced landing on Chicago's lakefront, in the era of aviation when engines were unreliable and smart pilots always had designated landing spots picked out in case of emergency. Above: A *Chicago Tribune* photo from the 1930s. Pierce "Scotty" O'Carroll flies his aircraft out of Soldier Field's parking lot after another pilot made an emergency landing there.

✈

Soldier Field was not the only place that Scotty O'Carroll had a forced landing. He also landed at Archer and Ashland Avenues, put a Stinson Reliant right on the beach adjacent to Jackson Park, and landed a Fledgling aircraft at 55th Street and the Midway Plaisance by the University of Chicago. When he attempted to fly out of Hyde Park, "the coppers wouldn't let him take it off," according to Mike Rezich.

Those pilots who could find a parking lot or a field were the lucky ones. Often in an emergency there was no place to land, and pilots had to rely on their instincts to survive.

Sheila O'Carroll Lynch relates another story of an emergency landing: "One time my father had a charter flight to Memphis. Something happened with the engine." It was at night, Fred Farbin continues, "We used to have flares in those days, usually three one-minute flares and one three-minute flare, which at night would light up the ground. Well, Scotty pulled the flares, and there were only two places to go—in the woods or in the river. So he put it in the river."

"He crashed his plane in the White River in Missouri," continues Sheila. "It was fairly deep and he had to get out of the plane fast. He didn't know how to swim, but he knew how to float. He was a very large man and he wore very heavy shoes; he took off his shoes and his clothes so they wouldn't weigh him down. He somehow floated across the river to the shore. He realized he had to get help, but he didn't have any clothes on and he couldn't swim to the

Above: A 1937 Gull A Stinson Reliant, owned and named *The Aristocratic Lady* by Pierce "Scotty" O'Carroll. The SR-10 was also nicknamed a "Gull Wing" because its wings were arrayed in a design similar to that of a sea gull in flight.

Right: The same SR-10 shown above, but obviously a lot wetter. O'Carroll ditched the plane in the White River in Missouri after his engine failed because he could not land in dense forest. O'Carroll and a co-pilot were not hurt and the plane was not severely damaged.

From the Lynch family collection.

From the Lynch family collection.

In the foreground of this aerial view is the Chicago Meadow Golf Course, to the north of the railroad tracks that bordered the airport along 59th Street. The golf course closed in 1934, and the land was later acquired by the city as expansion plans for the airport were put into motion.

clothes he took off. So he plastered mud and bits of leaves and branches around himself, and he walked until he found a farmhouse. The farmer's wife gave him her husband's overalls, many sizes too small, and he called my mother. She wired him money to buy clothes. I remember going with her to pick up my father at the station. I was about four years old."

With the arrival of WWII and the great increase in air travel came larger aircraft. The government realized that Municipal would have to increase the length of its runways. According to David Young, "just the possibility of increased use of four-engine aircraft like the DC-3 caused the city to double the airport's size." Before that it took up only the south half of Midway's current square-mile area.

From the Lynch family collection.

Workers excavate new runways for the expansion of Chicago Municipal Airport on the north side of the field on land that used to be the Chicago Meadows Golf Course, late 1930s.

There remained one problem—after runway expansion, the railroad tracks still ran down the middle of the world's busiest airport. These tracks were part of the main feeder line for the Belt Railroad and its yards, the largest in the country. The tracks had to be removed even though by law they had a perpetual right-of-way. The problem was solved when Washington, fearing that war was imminent, decided that Municipal Airport was needed for military operations. Congress enacted a special law and the tracks were relocated. In anticipation, runways and taxiways were paved on the land beyond the tracks, doubling

✈ 1934

The Chicago Meadows Golf Course goes out of business. This Northern section of land is immediately leased for the airport's use. The course's club house is moved to 57th Street and Central Avenue and becomes the home of John A. Casey, the airport manager.[6]

✈ 1935

Seven scheduled airlines operate from Chicago Municipal: American, Braniff, Eastern, Chicago and Southern, Northwest, Transcontinental & Western Air (TWA), and United Air Lines.[7]

8,000 employees are hired under a WPA (Work Progress Administration) grant from the federal government. At this time, more than 25% of all U.S. mail is handled in Chicago.

✈ 1936

One hundred thirteen scheduled flights leave Municipal daily.

The Douglas Aircraft Company introduces the DC-3, which would revolutionize passenger travel with its 21-passenger capacity and a cruising speed of 180 mph.[8]

✈ 1937–1939

Additional improvements are made to the airport, including sewers, lighting, parking, and the paving of the ramps and runways. In the ten years between 1929 and 1939, there were 697,407 flights at Municipal carrying over 2,190,769 passengers.[9]

Another airline, Pennsylvania Central, begins flights at Municipal, with service from Chicago to Washington and New York, bringing the total number of airlines operating at the field to eight.[10]

A poll in one of Chicago's newspapers asks its readership what they thought were the seven wonders of Chicago. Chicago Municipal ranked fourth, right after the Art Institute, Buckingham Fountain, and the Chicago Stock Yards.[11]

✈ 1940

Legal discussions begin to move the Chicago and Western Indiana Railroad tracks (also known as the Chicago Belt Railway) that bordered the airport at 59th Street.[12]

The tracks are removed on May 1, 1941, and rerouted to 55th Street. When aircraft began flying in the first decade of the twentieth century, railroads had little fear of any competition from the air. By 1941, railroad tracks being removed from an airport was an apt metaphor for how one mode of passenger travel could be overwhelmed by another.[13]

Poles and tracks for the streetcars that run along Cicero Avenue are removed between Archer Avenue and 63rd Street because they are considered an obstruction to aircraft. The trolley service is replaced by buses. The power company removes all electric poles and buries them, along with transformers, for the same reason.[14]

the size of the airport.

Chicago mayor Edward J. Kelly, airport manager John Casey, newspaper reporters and photographers, and the public watched as last train ran through the airport. The tracks were moved to 55th Street; the area was paved over; and on June 30, 1941, the airport, minus the railroad tracks, was dedicated.

"Almost before the concrete dried, the government began talking about building another airport. It eventually turned out to be O'Hare. The official studies of O'Hare date from after World War II, but they were talking about it even before they finished expanding Municipal Airport." [DY]

✈

1. John A. Casey, *Chicago Aviation and Airports: The First Forty Years, 1926-1966* (Chicago Department of Aviation report, 1966), 5.

2. Donald Herbert Donald, *Lincoln* (New York: Simon & Schuster, 1995), 250–1.

3. Robert M. Hill, *A Little Known Story of the Land Called Clearing* (Chicago: Chicago Historical Society, 1983), 197.

4. Ibid., 198.

5. Casey, 6.

6. Hill, 201.

7. Casey, 7.

8. Ibid., 8.

9. Hill, 202.

10. Casey, 8.

11. Richard White, *Remembering Ahanagran: Storytelling in a Family's Past* (New York: Hill and Wang, 1998), 232.

12. Casey, 8.

13. Hill, 208.

14. City of Chicago, Department of Public Works, *Annual Report*, 1941.

Courtesy of Robert F. Soraparu.

An aerial view of Chicago Municipal Airport, facing west, 1941. The expansion of the airport to the north is completed, and all that remains before the expanded runways can become operational is the removal of the railroad tracks from the center of the field.

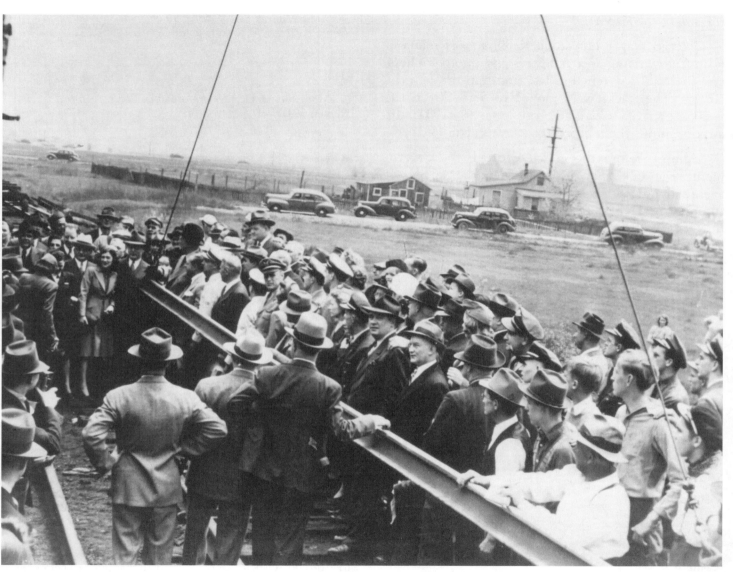

Courtesy of the City of Chicago, Department of Aviation.

The railroad tracks on the Belt Railway line that intersected Chicago Municipal Airport were removed on May 1, 1941, because longer runways were needed for heavier multi-engine aircraft of the era. The tracks were diverted north to run along 55th Street, and with the rails removed, an east-west runway, about a mile long, was laid over the abandoned railway bed. The building in the distance in the top right of the photo is the U.S. Army hangar for transient aircraft at Central Avenue and 60th Place.

From the Lynch family collection.

The new runways are complete on the north (right) side of the field, and a new east-west runway was paved over the railway bed that ran through the center of the field. With the longer runways, the airport was able to handle large military aircraft and traffic. Cicero Avenue is at the bottom of the photograph, while in the upper left hand corner, the Hale School can be seen right next to the tarmac.

Cropped from a map of Chicago by the H.M. Gousha Company, printed in What to See and Do in Chicago: 1940 Visitors' Guide (Created by the Brevoort Hotel). *Courtesy of Joshua Koppel.*

In the 1940s, there were still several smaller airports in the vicinity of Chicago Municipal Airport (top, center): Ashburn (bottom, right), Harlem (bottom, center), and Stinson (top, left).

THE AIRPORT GOES TO WAR: 1941-1945

On December 7, 1941, Pearl Harbor was attacked, and President Franklin D. Roosevelt declared war on Japan. Activity at Municipal increased as the military assumed supervision of air traffic control and took over the airline pilots and mechanics, issuing them uniforms. Runways, such as one 6,519 feet long, were long enough to handle the largest aircraft at the time, including the B-17 "Flying Fortress."

For young navy pilots, Chicago was a place of carrier training first and parties second. Charles Downey, the youngest naval aviator of World War II, recalls: "They put me in Chicago in Septem-

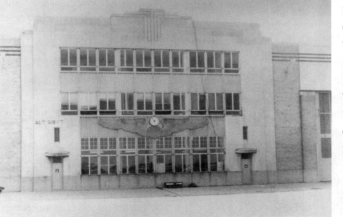

From the Lynch family collection.

The Air National hangar, built in 1935, seen from the tarmac at Chicago Municipal Airport.

ber of '43 for the first time. I learned all about the card game of twenty-one; I learned about the bars in Chicago, a great place. We were here about four days to execute the training that you received elsewhere and to demonstrate to the navy that you could make eight landings and not kill yourself or crash an airplane. I did that on the USS *Wolverine* and then went on to other squadron activity and combat on the USS *Ticonderoga* in the Pacific.

"The exercises took place in Lake Michigan. We had two Great Lakes passenger steamers converted to landing platforms by cutting off the top decks. They weren't

✈ June 30, 1941

The airport, without a railroad bisecting it, is dedicated; a new east-west runway rests on the abandoned bed of the removed railway tracks. To celebrate the completion, an airshow is held, with over 350,000 in attendance.[1]

✈ December 7, 1941

Pearl Harbor is attacked, and America declares war. Activity at Midway increases as the military assumes supervision of air traffic control. Runways, such as one that is 6,519 feet long, are large enough the handle the largest aircraft of the era, including the B-17 "Flying Fortress."[2]

Courtesy of Robert F. Zilinsky.

A military aircraft's wing taken during a training flight, 1940s.

✈ 1942

A B-17 crew member stationed at Municipal Airport in 1942 recalls that an aircraft based at the U.S. military's hangar for transient aircraft (60th Place and Central Avenue) was assigned to fly and pick up civilians at various air bases throughout the nation. What was unusual about these passengers was that their briefcases were handcuffed to their wrists as they were ferried by armed military escort from Municipal to the University of Chicago. The reason for these mysterious passengers became clear on December 2, 1942, when Enrico Fermi, Arthur Compton, and other scientists under Stagg Field unlocked the power of the atom with the first self-sustaining controlled nuclear reaction, giving birth to the Atomic Age.[3]

✈ June 30, 1942

Construction begins on Douglas Aircraft Corporation's newest plant, at Orchard Field, west of Chicago, which will build four-engine C-54s for the war effort. The runways, taxiways, and assembly plant are all completed by August 31, 1943. From 1943 to 1945, 655 C-54s are manufactured at this location.[4]

✈ 1944-1945

Airline passenger traffic at Chicago Municipal Airport exceeds the one million mark. American, TWA, and Pan American Airlines are all certified to provide service to several European cities, and Mayor Edward J. Kelly flies American Airlines' inaugural flight to London. The mayor uses this opportunity to lobby for the United Nations to establish itself in Chicago. Meanwhile, the neighborhoods around Midway continue to thrive with business and residential growth.[5]

A truck advertises war bonds at Chicago Municipal Airport during World War II.

✈ Women at Municipal Airport

During World War II, there was a shortage of men in many occupations at Chicago Municipal Airport. With the exception of the stewardesses, there were no women working in any official capacity in Chicago aviation, and airport officials felt the pressure to allow women to fill these vacant positions that were once the domain of men.

The first woman hired to work in the terminal was Valerie Foley, an immigrant from Ireland, for an entry-level position behind a counter. A half-century later, Erin O'Donnell, whose father came from Donegal, Ireland, became the first woman to serve as Midway's airport manager.[6]

✈ Sara Walsh

Sara Walsh, an Irish immigrant from County Kerry, got her first job at Chicago Municipal Airport in 1941 working at an information booth, from which she came into contact with many famous people over the years.

She remembers meeting Charles Lindbergh, who was flying on TWA (nicknamed, ironically enough, the Lindbergh Line). Sara also met Howard Hughes, the owner of TWA, who quizzed the young lady about the meaning of the initials of his airline. "Transcontinental and Western Air," she answered, which suited the multi-millionaire.

Eleanor Roosevelt would often be in the terminal, according to Sara, sitting at a lunch counter, away from the crowd. She once saw a cockroach try to climb onto the First Lady's plate.

But most importantly to Sara, the airport allowed her to mingle in a cosmopolitan crowd and to learn to like coffee: "I learned to be an American, really."[7]

The U.S. Army hangar for transient aircraft at Central Avenue and 60th Place. During World War II, it was the center of much activity with military aircraft arriving and departing.

From the Lynch family collection.

in any sense a carrier; they were moving platforms to take off from and land on. One plane at a time would occupy the deck during the landing and takeoff sequence. About fifteen thousand naval aviators demonstrated their ability to land and take off from a moving deck."

From the author's collection.

A painting of airport manager John Casey that ran in an electronics magazine and advertised two-way radios for operation, 1940s. Casey served as airport manager for decades, and during his tenure the airport went from a small airfield to the busiest airport in the world.

"There was quite an encampment of army aviation personnel on Central Avenue," Robert Hill remembers. "Once they had a chow line out there with a big tub of boiling water with hot dogs for the troops. The kids would climb the fence and take one look at those army guys and fliers, and the fliers would just keep shooting these hot dogs through the fence until the teachers and patrol boys told the kids, 'Leave those army guys alone!'"

One of the pilots that knew Chicago Municipal well was Jimmy Doolittle, who would make an historic contribution to aviation when his Doolittle Raiders made a raid on Tokyo shortly after the Japanese had bombed Pearl Harbor.

"I wrote to Jimmy Doolittle a few years ago, and I thanked him for what he did," said Downey. "He was one of my heroes, along with Lindbergh."

Tom Goldthorpe places Doolittle in the pantheon of aviation's heroes: "You might say that of the top innovators—the Wright Brothers, Lindbergh, and Doolittle, it would be Doolittle that established a utility for air travel that heretofore had not been done. Doolittle didn't invent instruments per se, but he established the technique of instrument flying. He was the first to virtually fly blind in clouds from point A to point B.

"He got in trouble many times. He was at Kelly Field in Texas in 1918 or 1919. He made a bet with another flying officer that he could, while in flight, climb out of the old biplane, go out on the wing and from there onto the lower landing gear, squat on the axle, and hang on to the side braces

Robert Hill
is the author of the valuable book, *A Little Known Story of the Land Called Clearing*, an exceptional look at the Clearing District and the major role that the airport and aviation had on that area.

Airplanes parked at Chicago Municipal Airport during World War II. Left: A Seversky P-35A. Above, left: An Advanced Trainer (AT-1) in front of the U.S. Army hangar. Above, right: A North American BT-9A in front of the U.S. Army hangar.

Courtesy of Robert F. Zilinsky.

Airplanes parked at Chicago Municipal Airport during World War II. From the very beginning of Municipal the military had aircraft stationed there. Above: A Douglas B-18A "Bolo," on the ramp in front of the U.S. Army hangar. Above, right: An army Boeing 80 aircraft, the same type of plane that flew passengers in the early 1930s. Right: A Douglas O38B in front of the U.S. Army hangar.

Courtesy of Robert F. Zilinsky.

James Doolittle, an air racer, visited Chicago Municipal Airport frequently during the 1930s when he worked for Shell Oil. Later, during the first few months of World War II, he led the "Doolittle Raiders" on their daring raid over Japan.

der, and when he saw the young pilot in the distance clinging to the landing gear, he jumped up and screamed, 'Get me Doolittle!' When his adjutant said he was unclear who the officer was, the commander said, 'No one would pull a crazy stunt like that except Doolittle.'

"In his youth, Doolittle became famous as an air racer. During the 1930s, he was one of the few pilots who successfully flew the notorious Gee Bee, a tiny plane that had about eight hundred horsepower. It was designed and built by the Granville Brothers out of Massachusetts, hence the name Gee Bee. It was a traitorous little plane and a lot of people got themselves killed in it. Doolittle flew it to victory, and afterwards reporters asked him why he chose to fly that airplane knowing its reputation as a man killer. Doolittle answered simply, 'Because it's the fastest!'"

After World War II, Chicago showed its appreciation for the soldiers and sailors who had fought so valiantly for their country by renaming Chicago Municipal Airport Chicago Midway Airport after the naval battle that practically turned the tide of the war in the Pacific. It was a gesture that meant a great deal to the returning GIs.

✈

while the other guy landed the plane. While acting out the $5 wager, unbeknown to Doolittle, Cecil B. DeMille and a film crew were shooting footage of army aircraft for a movie. DeMille saw Doolittle out on the axle and filmed the whole stunt. Later that evening, the rushes were shown to the base comman-

1. City of Chicago, Department of Public Works, *Annual Report*, 1941.

2. Robert M. Hill, *A Little Known Story of the Land Called Clearing* (Chicago: Chicago Historical Society, 1983), 208.

3. Ibid.

4. John A. Casey, *Chicago Aviation and Airports: The First Forty Years, 1926-1966* (Chicago Department of Aviation report, 1966), 12.

5. Ibid., 11.

6. Richard White, *Remembering Ahanagran: Storytelling in a Family's Past* (New York: Hill and Wang, 1998), 232.

7. Ibid., 234.

Gooney Birds and Midway Island

During World War II, military pilots stationed on Midway Island in the Pacific began to call DC-3s "Gooney Birds," because the planes, so awkward-looking on the ground, reminded them of the fledgling albatrosses that populated Midway Island.

Ironically, Chicago Municipal, where these metal gooney birds populated the tarmac, would be renamed in honor of the battle that took place near Midway Island, the refuge of the gooney bird.

In 1992, to celebrate the fiftieth anniversary of the Battle of Midway, the airport hosted a fly-in of World War II-era warbirds, such as this P-51 Mustang.

Courtesy of Harold Lind.

After World War II, construction for a larger terminal for Chicago Municipal Airport began. The girders for the new tower are being erected.

From the author's collection.

Courtesy of Robert F. Soraparu.

Chicago Municipal Airport, early 1950s, before concourses were added to the terminal.

Part III

Boom and Bust

1945–1963

✈

The observation promenade was a popular place to view airplanes at Chicago Midway Airport and lucrative for the city, 1952.

✈ CROSSROADS OF THE WORLD

The frenzied activity that World War II brought to Chicago's airport did not cease when peace came. On the contrary, it became busier than ever at Chicago's newly-named Midway Airport.

Retired commercial and corporate pilot Philip Felper relates: "It was really busy. Eastern Airlines and some of the others had a plane approaching or taking off every few minutes. If the weather got bad, you had yourself a real job. The approach came right over the top of the end hangar on the field, the American Airlines hangar, and if you wanted a thrill you'd be in that hangar; when you heard the engines running like hell when the weather was bad, you'd run out to a side of the hangar. I'm surprised that nobody hit the hangar. But that's the way it was in this busiest airport in the world.

"This was one of the best fields in the country to land at because you had a place to eat, you could get people to work on your airplane, get fuel. For fun, there was that fella Roscoe Turner who carried a

full-grown lion with him, and he stopped at Chicago many times, and he'd come off his plane with the lion. It kept you away from his plane, anyhow."

Midway was fast becoming the center of aviation in the United States, but there were still some issues that had to be addressed. Since 1926, the City of

A photograph of the Nathan Hale elementary school, 1940s. The school was approximately 100 yards from an active runway of the busiest airport in the world at the time.

From the Lynch family collection.

✈ August 21, 1945

Due to expanding air traffic at Municipal, Mayor Kelly appoints a Site Location Committee to recommend sites for a second airport. The committee selects Douglas Airport, also known as Orchard Place, located west of Mannheim Road and south of Higgins Road on the city's Northwest Side.[1]

✈ March 22, 1946

The City of Chicago acquires 1,080 acres of the Douglas site, which includes a small hangar. The military retains the assembly plant and other structures on the field.[2]

✈ 1946

Robert Platt, writes a report for the Association of American Geographers on the Clearing District and mentions the peculiar location of the Hale School, which, because of airport expansion, is a few feet from an active runway at Midway.

There are now ten scheduled airlines operating at Municipal with the addition of Trans-Canada Airlines. Delta moved to the field the year before. Ramps are widened at the airport to accommodate larger aircraft such as the DC-4.

Cicero Avenue is widened to an eight-lane highway.[3]

✈ May 3, 1946

TWA begins service to London. Municipal now has several carriers going to Europe. Still, the range of aircraft of the day prevent direct flights. A flight from Chicago to London takes place in hops from Chicago; New York; Montreal; Gander Bay or Goose Bay, Newfoundland; and across the Atlantic to Shannon Ireland.

✈ 1947

Parents with children at the Hale School petition the school board to move the school. Before a new school can be built elsewhere, however, something must be done in the interim about airplanes so close to the school.

Courtesy of Robert F. Soraparu.

Passengers board from the rear door of a United Air Lines DC-4 at Chicago Municipal Airport, 1947.

Passengers prepare to board the TWA Lockheed 049 Constellation *Star of Cairo* at Chicago, late 1940s.

Because Sheila O'Carroll's parents spent so much time at the airport, most of the photos taken of her as a child have her posing in front of airplanes. Left: Pierce O'Carroll with his daughter, Sheila, early 1940s. Above: Sheila and Pierce O'Carroll (far right) with friends in front of a Monarch Air Service DC-3 at Midway Airport, 1940s. Right: Sheila O'Carroll Lynch as a toddler.

From the Lynch family collection

Chicago had leased Midway from the Board of Education. Consequently, for the next 20 years, Hale Grammar School shared its land with the airport.

In the beginning, when Midway was in its infancy, there was little concern about this rather unusual arrangement. But as the field expanded, and the world's most active runways ran right next to the school, parents and administrators began to get uneasy. For pilots like Felper it was about time. "There was a large school [Hale] right down here on the corner of 63rd and Central just on the airport side. When all the kids came out for recess they'd come running out where the airplanes would be flying around 'em. It was a strange setup but the Board of Education didn't seem to worry too much."

In 1946, Robert Platt, hired by the Association of American Geographers for the Clearing District, wrote a report that highlighted the Hale School's peculiar location a few feet from a working runway after airport expansion. Platt wrote that "when the wind is easterly, planes warm up by the school making noise, when westerly, they fly over it."[4]

According to Robert Hill, a Hale alum, students in the classrooms could hear airplanes revving their engines before takeoff, and students "could hear the window glass hum, see the ink in your inkwell ripple, and feel the room vibrate.[5]

"They wanted to close Hale School down because of all the noise around it. The parents went to the Board of Education who told them they'd close the school and get the kids into schools that were a lot quieter. The parents started realizing that their kids were going to get split up into different schools because the Board was not going to build another school for them. The parents complained again. The Board said you're the ones who wanted to close the school because of the noise and that's what we're going to do.

"The parents kept up the pressure until Mayor Martin J. Kennelley said 'the children come first ahead of big business. Hale School will stay open until a new school is built.'

"And the arrangement that was made was incredible. The two runways that straddled Hale School were to be closed for the hours that the children were in school. They might just as well put up street signs saying 'No airplanes may use the prevailing runways of the busiest airport in the world on school days when children are present.' It's unbelievable but it sure made them hurry up and build a new school."

There was not much public flying until after World War II. It was very expensive; only the wealthy and many movie stars flew as a substitute for the streamliners—first class train travel.

Sheila Lynch talks about her dad's early charters. "He took many entertainers, like Orson Welles and Ingrid Bergman, because they were among the few who could afford to hire a plane all to themselves to play vaudeville in some small town or watch other acts. He also did a certain amount of factory work, a lot in Janesville, Wisconsin. I can remember going with him and carrying a small box of nuts that were important to one of the factories because the assembly line would have to shut down if they ran out of

Los Angeles Times

PLANE WRECK PROVES PLOT

Pilot Confesses Being Hired by Rival in Air Taxi Business to Smash Craft

CHICAGO, Feb. 8. (AP)—"Y'see," said Edward Kennedy, "I was hired to crack up that airplane of yours so you wouldn't have any more airplane taxi business."

"I see," said Pierce O'Carroll, reminiscently caressing his jaw and noting that all his front teeth are gone.

The colloquy took place at the detective station and from it this developed:

O'Carroll had been a partner of Dewey B. Biggs in a flying taxi service, but when he had a chance to buy, cheap, a dual control plane, he bought. It became the O'Carroll aerial taxi and aviation school.

One day a man named Casey wanted to learn how to fly. He took a few lessons and then the O'Carroll plane sideslipped from 100 feet up and smashed into little bits. Casey, unhurt, vanished. O'Carroll lost his front teeth. That set him sleuthing.

Today he had brought about the arrest of Kennedy as "Casey," and police obtained a confession. Likewise, Biggs and Christ Hedd, who works for Biggs, are in jail—all charged with malicious mischief.

"I got $50 from Hedd for the job," said Kennedy, "—but nothing extra for knocking out his teeth."

From the Lynch family collection.

The story of the conspiracy to wreck O'Carroll's plane by former business partner Dewey Biggs made the *Los Angeles Times*, 1931.

From the Lynch family collection.

A business card for Illinois Flying School, based at Ashburn Field from about 1930. Dewey Biggs was the manager and Pierce O'Carroll the flight instructor. When O'Carroll quit to form his own school, Biggs hired someone to try to sabotage O'Carroll's new business by crashing one of O'Carroll's planes.

these particular nuts. It was worth it to them to fly in just a box of nuts."

Even though aviation was still a relatively small part of American transportation, competition for business, even from flight students, was ruthless. Another man with a flying school felt that O'Carroll was taking too many students away from him. He arranged for an accident when Scotty was flying. O'Carroll's plane was badly damaged and many of his teeth were knocked out, but he survived. The perpetrators were caught, tried, and sentenced. The brutal competition between airlines and charters fighting for passengers and freight soon spread to other forms of transportation.

Airlines hurt the railroads by co-opting first-class travel. The bulk of passenger profit for the train industry came from wealthy people buying Pullman compartments. When it was discovered that flying from Chicago to New York was inexpensive and faster than taking the train, the public's wariness towards flying slowly began to evaporate.

Phil Felper, who flew for American Airlines, recalls that era. "They thought we were a little nuts, but there's a lot of people that get excited with airplanes. And then of course when they found that they could fly an airplane, to New York for instance, for $29.95, how can you compete with that? And you were there in four hours! And you know, that was fast. My God, you'd be a fool to go any other way. And you got lunch. A sandwich, an apple, and a piece of cake!"

Pilots called the Chicago to New York corridor "Thunder Alley" due to the frequency of storms on that run. In turbulent air, a complementary sandwich was not always too appealing, because as Felper adds, "You threw it up right away. And the stewardesses—

we called them 'stews' then—would come up there and say 'You bastards'! That was their friendly name for the pilots. And the stew would say, 'You know how many people you've gotten sick?' I'd say, 'How many?' And she'd say, 'About twenty-nine.' I'd say, 'What the hell, we've got 75 passengers! What are you complaining about?'"

At first, airlines only offered first-class service at first-class fares—only one charge until after World War II. David Young: "In 1947 tourist fares were introduced by some airlines with surplus DC-4s trying to sell seats. If any remained empty before a scheduled flight, they'd be offered at lower 'tourist' prices. The idea spread like wildfire."

And just like after World War I, a lot of cheap planes became available after World War II. Enterprising business people bought surplus military and

transport aircraft and started airlines on a shoestring, providing inexpensive seats. These were the small, independent non-scheduled airlines, the "non-skeds."

Entrepreneurs such as O'Carroll bought the surplus aircraft and started operation. The federal government had no interstate commerce law regulating these large planes as non-scheduled carriers. Any person who could buy the modestly-priced ticket, including servicemen coming home on leave and blue-collar workers with factory jobs, could fly to Florida or California in a matter of hours instead of having to drive for days.

O'Carroll began his non-sked carrier after purchasing a DC-3 from American Airlines in 1947 and then acquiring two C-47s and three C-46s. Fred Farbin, who flew co-pilot on many of Monarch's non-sked flights, looked back on that era. "It was

CHECK THIS TABLE OF COMPARATIVE COSTS

HOW TO SAVE TIME AND $$$	Time Best Ground Time	C & S AIR TIME	TIME SAVED	CASH AIR FARE	*Cost Best Gr'nd Travel	TRAVEL PLAN FARE	MONEY SAVED BY AIR
CHICAGO to ST. LOUIS	4 hrs. 55 min.	1 hr. 40 min.	3 hrs. 15 min.	$12.95	$12.57	$11.00	$ 1.57
NEW ORLEANS to CHICAGO	20 hours	6 hrs. 20 min.	13 hrs. 40 min.	46.64	47.27	39.64	7.63
HOUSTON TO CHICAGO	25 hrs. 15 min.	7 hrs. 5 min.	18 hrs. 10 min.	54.63	49.87	46.43	3.44
ST. LOUIS to MEMPHIS	7 hrs. 25 min.	1 hr. 40 min.	5 hrs. 45 min.	13.93	15.00	11.84	3.16
JACKSON to MEMPHIS	4 hrs. 33 min.	1 hr. 15 min.	3 hrs. 18 min.	10.15	11.18	8.62	2.56
SHREVEPORT to ST. LOUIS	14 hrs. 50 min.	3 hrs. 40 min.	11 hrs. 10 min.	29.48	26.11	25.05	1.06

*Ground Fares include Railroad Ticket, Extra Fare, Pullman, Meals and Tips. No Meals to Buy When You Fly—No Tips. One way fares quoted.

An ad from Chicago and Southern Airlines, highlighting why flying made more economic sense than taking the train, late 1940s.

From the author's collection.

*Courtesy of
David E. Kent
and Bill Aitken.*

A TWA
Constellation in the
intersection of 63rd
Street and Cicero
Avenue, December
8, 1949. The TWA
aircraft, *Star of the
Persian Gulf*, came
in too fast while
landing at Midway
Airport and skidded
off the runway and
through a fence
before coming to a
stop. There were
no injuries. It is
reported that one
overzealous police
officer attempted
to give the pilot
a parking ticket.[6]

The snack shop at Chicago Municipal Airport's first terminal building, 6200 S. Cicero Avenue,
where travelers could enjoy a sandwich for 50 cents, 1946.

✈ A Chicago Aviation Original: Edward Daly ✈

One of the many colorful characters who got their start at Midway was Edward Daly, born in 1922 to an Irish firefighting family from the South Side of Chicago. He learned about life from boxing in Golden Gloves tournaments, then from serving in the Pacific during World War II. He returned to Chicago and worked at Chicago Municipal Airport for the non-scheduled airlines, including Monarch Air Service, that were so popular after the war. The maverick non-skeds were no doubt a happy fit for Daly, such a renegade himself.

A love for flying brought Daly's involvement with a California charter business, World Airways, of which he was able to acquire a share. Over the succeeding decades, the Oakland-based airline continued to grow, with Daly eventually at the helm.

During the Vietnam War era, most of World Airways' business came from flying military personnel to Southeast Asia. On March 29, 1975, the South Vietnam city of Da Nang began falling to the North Vietnamese; World Airways had a contract with the U.S. military to fly twenty evacuation flights to the beleaguered city. Due to the extreme danger of the missions, the military suspended the contract after just three flights.

Daly, however, who had seen such suffering when visiting Hungarian refugee camps in 1956, refused to give in and personally ordered a World Airways 727 to fly in and rescue as many women and children as possible. When the jet landed, Daly was deluged by a crush of panicked people desperate to get aboard. He drew on his Golden Gloves training and punched those who rushed the plane's door, even using his pistol to whack the heads of anyone trying to push past.

The crowd became so large that the runway was all but impassable, and pilot Ken Healy instead raced the plane down a 5,000-foot taxiway, as soldiers fired bullets and launched grenades at the jet, one of which exploded and damaged the aircraft. The 727 continued on its takeoff roll, hitting a pole as it gathered speed. Even with the overcapacity of 350 passengers aboard, including eight people clinging inside the landing gear compartment, the jet's nose lifted off and the plane limped into the air. Thanks to Daly's commitment, the flight and the innocent caught in the midst of war would make it. In 1984, Edward Daly died, a true humanitarian and a tough fighter who learned to apply in life the boxer's trick of keeping out of the corners and off the ropes.[7]

---

going pretty good except you ran into a lot of problems trying to fill the airplanes up. We were going to Miami, Seattle, New York, and Los Angeles (an eight-hour trip in a DC-3). We also had a contract with the U.S. Department of Immigration to fly the illegal aliens back to San Antonio, Texas."

Farbin recounted that the scheduled airlines, like American and United, "all had their routes governed—where they could go and what they could charge. We [the non-scheduled airlines] were the new guy on the block. We couldn't leave at a certain time because then we would be classified as a scheduled carrier. We didn't have the expenses the airlines had, so we could charge a much lower fare, like twenty-four dollars to New York."

Yet the non-skeds had their own problems.

"When you're flying that kind of equipment and trying to keep up with the Big Guy, it's tough to maintain the airplanes properly. It's go, go, go, go,

UNSCHEDULED AIRLINES

Big business is not so stuck on private enter-prise when it benefits the small businessman

and beat the next guy out, and beat his price. Somewhere along the line, the work is not being done the way it should be done.

"And the non-skeds started having a terrible record. I mean, practically every week you'd pick up the paper and one of them was crashing, and the majority was contributed to just crew training and 'tired iron,' and trying to keep it going and make a dollar at the same time." [FF]

Monarch not only flew their own non-sked airline, but serviced others as well. Many of these visiting non-skeds did not pay their bills. Farbin would listen to a scanner at work—and even at home—and if he heard the tail number of a particular deadbeat carrier, he'd make sure that upon landing, two Monarch fuel trucks would be there to block the aircraft until payment was received.

In one instance, to be on the safe side, Monarch removed the battery from the plane of a known credit risk. Farbin wanted to box the plane in with the fuel trucks just to be even safer, but Scotty O'Carroll thought that such an action wasn't necessary. That night, the plane's crew jumped the fence with a new battery and, with no fuel trucks in the way, took off, much to O'Carroll's annoyance.

"When you flew the non-skeds with the seventy-two passengers, you had uniforms that were gorgeous," says Phil Felper. "You had more braid than a general, and you'd walk up the aisle with those hats and big wings on your jacket, and you'd smile at everybody, and they thought you were God. You'd smile twice at the pretty girls and get the number of their seats."

Sheila Lynch: "The government didn't approve of

Courtesy of Robert F. Soraparu.

Left: A woman and child enjoy the view of the airport from the Midway Airport terminal promenade, 1950.
According to a 1949 annual report, the observation deck generated $25,633.30 in revenue from concessions.
Right: The view of the tarmac at Midway Airport, as a flight attendant awaits passenger boarding at Midway, mid-1950s.

Courtesy of Robert F. Soraparu.

An aerial view of Midway's Terminal at 5700 S. Cicero in the early 1950s.

An ad for Pierce "Scotty" O'Carroll's non-scheduled airline. The inexpensive non-skeds proved so popular that they began to hurt scheduled commercial airline service.

From the Lynch family collection.

FLY
$39 To $39
MIAMI
with
"SCOTTY" O'CARROLL
for $39 Tax Extra
TAMPA_____ $39
Hotel Rates Reduced Apr. 15
25 Years Air Charter & Sight-
seeing Experience in Chicago
THE oldest complete Air Service
in the Nation.
MONARCH AIR SERVICE
POrtsmouth 7-1515
(Travel Agents Recognized)

the non-skeds and wanted to regulate them because they were in direct competition with regular commercial airlines like United, American, and Pan-American, who felt that the non-skeds were biting too much into their business."

"The government decided to regulate non-sked aviation; in fact, it almost strangled the industry to death. They stopped them because they were doing so well, they were knocking the hell out of the regular airlines." [PF]

Scotty O'Carroll was so upset with the government's interference with the non-skeds, he wrote letters to government agencies in Washington and appeared before the Senate Committee that was dealing with the issue. Not being shy, O'Carroll also wrote a letter to President Harry Truman in 1950. He wrote that from the moment he stepped off the boat from Ireland, "I was fired with ambition to make a name for myself in the great United States," and that from the moment he had received

his pilot's license, "from that day to this, my whole thought, word, and deeds were for the good of aviation."

O'Carroll observed that the dream of open and free competition in the skies was beginning to erode because of government interference, and that the public would suffer the most from such bureaucratic intrusions. He said he felt this was in direct opposition to the dream of inexpensive air travel. He relayed how he had spent the last "twenty-five years of the best part of a man's life devoted to an idea—progress in aviation to provide air transportation to the working man, his wife, and family. I feel proud to be able to provide low-cost air transportation."

Such competition, O'Carroll reiterated, "gave the working man air transportation at low cost. Let's all work to provide air transportation at low cost, even lower than at present, if possible. It's the American way of life."

There is no record of a response from Washington. The regulatory climate became so unfavorable to the non-skeds that O'Carroll got out of the business in 1951. His dream of cheap fares for the common person had stalled.

"Gradually, the non-skeds did go out of business because of the regulations, but the regulated airlines adopted many of the ideals that the non-skeds began. The non-skeds were the beginning of passenger flight as we know it now, where almost everyone can say he or she has had the opportunity to fly." [SL]

David Young suggests that the non-skeds were

"really the forerunners of what are the interstate carriers at Midway, like Southwest Airlines, which now dominate the airport. But, their time wasn't right earlier because aviation was so financially shaky."

"You were regulated to death," according to Charles Downey. "The government even told us what kind of snack service we could provide. They shouldn't have been able to regulate everything."

Tom Goldthorpe concurs, "I don't think the government really wanted to understand aviation. They wanted power, to use aviation to sustain itself. If the government had regulated Chanute and the Wrights when they were experimenting, the airplane would have never been invented."

"Then you also have the charter operators coming along afterwards. It was the same idea as the non-skeds, somebody would have a tour going somewhere, and instead of hiring a bigwig airline with a scheduled carrier, they could get much cheaper service if they chartered another aircraft." [DY]

"That's the way the same guys got around the

The observation deck was a popular place to watch airplanes at Midway Airport.

Courtesy of Marshall Field's.

SHORTEST DISTANCE BETWEEN 2 POINTS

NEW SPEED TO SHORTEN THE DISTANCE

QUIET LUXURY TO MAKE THE TIME FLY

Largest, Roomiest Airliner in the World
Far Quieter for Greater Comfort • Wider Aisles
Larger Windows • Wider Seats
Finest Air Conditioning • Restful 5-Cabin Privacy
Congenial Starlight Lounge
Interior Design by Henry Dreyfuss
The Fastest Constellation Ever Built.

non-sked problem when they were regulated out of business. They went into the charter business," Sheila Lynch explains. "A lot of the military used charters. Remember, this was after World War II and around the time of the Korean War. So you had an awful lot of military people traveling with their wives and dependents, and other kinds of people, just for weekends."

✈

1. John A. Casey, *Chicago Aviation and Airports: The First Forty Years, 1926-1966* (Chicago Department of Aviation report, 1966), 11.

2. Ibid., 12.

3. Ibid.

4. Robert M. Hill, *A Little Known Story of the Land Called Clearing* (Chicago: Chicago Historical Society, 1983), 220.

5. Ibid.

6. Peter J. Marson, *The Lockheed Constellation Series* (Air Britain Publication, 1982).

7. Jeff S. Johnson, "World's Colorful Past," *Airliners Magazine*, Sept./Oct. 1994. Also, World Airways Web site, www.worldair.com, accessed 6 August 2001.

An ad for the Super Constellation shows that it wasn't only Pullman cars on trains that guaranteed luxury, but air travel as well.

From the author's collection.

Courtesy of Robert F. Soraparu.

A Capital
Airlines
Lockheed 749
Constellation
on the tarmac of
Chicago Midway
Airport, 1952.

Although today the Department of Aviation is a large and separate city agency, it was not always so. Aviation matters were originally handled by the Department of Public Works and did not even warrant its own bureau, but rather was part of the Bureau of Parks, Recreation and Aviation. Old annual reports from the Department of Public Works reveal aviation sections hardly more than a page long, sandwiched between reports on forestry and playgrounds. There was some logic placing aviation within the jurisdiction of the Bureau of Parks; in the early days of aviation, a park was the only place in the city of Chicago that a plane could land, and in 1911, Grant Park specifically.

A Braniff DC-6 over 55th Street and Cicero Avenue as it makes it approach to Runway 22L at Midway Airport, 1955.

Courtesy of Robert F. Soraparu.

A view of the American Airlines concourse from the Midway Control Tower, 1950s.

A view of the tarmac, with the tower. The Marshall Field's Cloud Room can be seen on the second floor.

✈ The Cloud Room: A Taste of Marshall Field's at Midway

idway was becoming more than just the busiest airport in the world during the 1940s and '50s. It had developed beyond being merely a transportation hub into a social center and form of entertainment, particularly for residents of the city's Southwest Side. Crowds visited the airport every day and lined up against the fence or perched atop the observation deck to watch the airplanes take off and land. Afterwards, thanks to Marshall Field's, they could have a fine meal.

Even though Municipal was a world-class airport before it was "Midway," it lacked world-class dining. Hungry travelers might get a hot dog or a cup of coffee if they could stomach it, but food accommodations at the terminal were primitive at best.

Chicago mayor Edward Kelly eventually asked Hughston McBain, president of Marshall Field's, to take over the concessions stand at the airport, and McBain agreed. The construction in 1948 of a new terminal north of the old terminal yielded more room

Courtesy of Marshall Field's.

Another view of Marshall Field's Cloud Room, as seen from the tarmac.

✈ 1947–1948

The new terminal is completed. United Air Lines moves in and traffic is controlled from the new tower. A new 300-car parking lot is built, with parking costing 25 cents for four hours. On March 18, 1948, Marshall Field's opens the Cloud Room restaurant and the Blue and Gold Cafe.

✈ June 22, 1949

The City Council renames Orchard Field, northwest of Chicago, after Edward "Butch" O'Hare, a naval aviator killed during World War II, and changes Municipal's name to Midway in honor of World War II's Battle of Midway. The ordinance goes into effect a couple weeks later on July 8.[1]

✈ 1950

Midway Airport receives a Class I rating from the Civil Aeronautics Authority. Fifteen scheduled airlines are now servicing Midway Airport.[2]

In addition to the scheduled flights, there are non-scheduled ones, and their arrival on the transportation scene is not universally welcomed. The non-skeds prove popular with young honeymooners and families, many of whom take their first vacations on an airplane. The more established airlines, whose businesses are being undercut by these cheap flights, successfully lobby Congress to regulate the non-skeds out of business.

✈ 1951

The city erects a sign at the airport that declares "Midway Airport: Cross-roads of the World," entirely accurate considering the international dignitaries that arrive at Midway in this era. India's first prime minister Jawaharlal Nehru flew into Midway in 1949; General Douglas MacArthur and future Israeli prime minister Golda Meir flew in during 1951.[3]

✈ 1952

Passenger traffic at Midway reaches the five million mark.

✈ 1955

The location of the Hale School, so close to an active runway, continues to cause considerable worry and problems for both parents of students, as well as air traffic controllers and pilots. Mayor Martin Kennelly, outraged by the situation, declares that "our children come first and big business second," leading to the extraordinary order to close the two busiest runways between 8:30 A.M. and 3:30 P.M. on school days at the busiest airport in the world.[4] The Hale School is demolished by November 22, 1955.[5]

✈ October 29, 1955

Its passenger terminal completed, passenger service begins at O'Hare Field.[6]

✈ 1956

Helicopter operations among Midway, O'Hare, and Meigs Field begin. Nineteen scheduled air carriers are serving Midway.

✈ 1958

Airlines operating this year at Midway Airport include Air France, American, Braniff, Delta, Eastern, Lake Central, North Central, Ozark, Riddle, TWA, Airlift International, BOAC, Capitol, Chicago Helicopter, Flying Tiger, Lufthansa, Northwest, Pan American, Trans Canada, and United.[7]

Military operations on the field include the headquarters of the Illinois Air National Guard, the headquarters of the 126th Fighter Interceptor Wing, the 126th Air Base Group, and the 108th Fighter Interceptor Squadron.[8]

With the advent of the four-engine aircraft and later the commercial jet, Midway Airport begins to show its constraints. Though jet aircraft technology is shrinking both time and distance, runways needed for these advanced aircraft have to be longer. Midway Airport, with its limited size, is seen as too small for the expanding technology, and calls for another airport begin. It is this transition from Midway to a small airstrip called Old Orchard that begins the dominion of O'Hare Airport.

for dining facilities. On March 18, 1948, Marshall Field's Cloud Room opened. At the grand opening were Kelly's successor, Mayor Martin J. Kennelly; James L. Palmer, executive president of Marshall Field's; and W. A. Patterson, president of United Air Lines. Living up to the maxim "make no small plans," the celebration included a live radio broadcast on WENR called "Wagon Wheels to Wings," and a TV program on WBKB.

The Cloud Room represented elegance and style. Diners entered through two glass doors on the first floor of the terminal. The restaurant was on the second floor, where large windows offered guests a panoramic view of the airplanes below on the tarmac. One reporter wrote that "in contrast to the excitement outside the window, there is a calm relaxation inside the handsome, air-conditioned dining room. Overhead in one corner, a large abstract gold-colored mobile swings in lazy circles."[9] That mobile was *Flight in Motion*, created by famed sculptor Alexander Calder.

The Cloud Room brought a luxury to air travel unfamiliar to most airports of the day, an experience closer to that of traveling in Pullman railroad cars. It was an immediate success and attracted 1.25 million visitors annually. It soon hosted, according to its visitor's book, not only travelers from places as distant as Hong Kong, Capetown, and the Congo, but Hollywood celebrities such as Clark Gable, Van Johnson, Burt Lancaster, Jack Benny, Bob Hope, and James Stewart, and other notables like William Randolph Hearst, Jr. and former first lady Eleanor

Courtesy of Marshall Field's.

A mobile created by Alexander Calder, *Flight in Motion*, was displayed in Marshall Field's Cloud Room.

Roosevelt.

But dining at the Cloud Room wasn't only for the rich and famous. Families from Chicago often dressed up on a Sunday morning to have brunch there, as the children enjoyed watching the airplanes arrive and depart. Colorful menus highlighted the latest trendy fare. No matter how fancy the menus became, however, the Chicken Pot Pie, made with flaky puff pastry, was the perennial favorite.

To keep up with the countless diners and ensure the operation ran smoothly twenty-four hours a day, Marshall Field's employed 180 kitchen and wait staffers. An informal eatery, the Blue and Gold Cafe,

Left: The entrance to Marshall Field's acclaimed Cloud Room restaurant on the second floor of the terminal at Midway Airport.

Above: Artwork from a Cloud Room menu.

Courtesy of Marshall Field's.

Courtesy of Robert F. Soraparu.

The Cloud Room offered visitors to Midway an elegant dining experience, along with a wonderful view of aircraft on the tarmac.

Courtesy of Marshall Field's.

The Blue and Gold Cafe, also operated by Marshall Field's, had a panoramic view of the airport's tarmac and served customers 24 hours a day.

was located below the Cloud Room, for travelers who wanted a quick bite. It was the kind of place where waitresses called you "Honey" and the coffee flowed constantly, and it had the same fantastic view of the planes on the tarmac. For those with a flight to catch, the cafe began serving an "Air Lunch Box" in 1950, a different take on airplane food.

In the May 31, 1949, edition of Field's employee newsletter, *Field Glass*, the author notes a new type of customer beginning to be known at the airport:

> A large portion of America's small fry has taken to the air in recent years. They are accompanied by anxious mothers bearing a vast assortment of 'formula bottles,' talcum powder, and three-cornered pieces of cloth. These babies, it seems, are quite 'air-worthy' for they get along better (in flight) than many grownups. Babies cry less, wiggle less, but suck their thumbs more while they are in an airplane than they do in the security of their cribs at home. But there is one drawback. Babies, for all their good behavior in the air, still continue to suffer 'misfortunes,' which must be taken care of on the ground many times.
>
> That's where Airport Restaurants people re-enter the picture. For fate seems determined that all baby formula bottles be empty when the planes touch the ground and that the arrival of any baby in Chicago must be heralded by a complete change of diapers.
>
> Thus Field employees at the airport have adapted the very workable slogan of America's Boy Scouts—'Be Prepared.'[10]

For all that air travel has changed in the new millennium, try finding baby formula at a major metropolitan airport these days.

Unfortunately, as Midway's passenger service de-

clined, so did the Cloud Room. It closed up shop in 1962 after fourteen years of feeding Midway's travelers. Still, in that short period, Marshall Field's proved that dining at an airport could be elegant and, like their Christmas windows on State Street, an experience that one could look forward to enjoying again and again.

Sheila Lynch looks back on those years: "My father (Scotty O'Carroll) gave rides over the city in the '40s and '50s. He flew the sightseers for $3.50 a ride, three to four at a time depending on how much

Mrs. Henry Thyer, winner of the South Berwyn Chamber of Commerce's "Luckiest Mother" contest, Mothers Day, 1949. Her prizes included dining at the Cloud Room and an aerial tour of Chicago by Scotty O'Carroll.

Photo by Mike Rotunno. Courtesy of the family of Mike Rotunno.

✈ Photographer to the Stars: Mike Rotunno

When celebrities passed through Midway Airport during its heyday as an aviation crossroads, Mike Rotunno was there to capture them on film. A photographer at the airport from the 1920s to the 1980s, he used his humor, winning personality, and persistence to photograph the stars for the newspapers, chronicling an exciting piece of Midway's history in the process and becoming a legend in his own right.

Rotunno grew up in the Italian neighborhood near Taylor and Halsted Streets, a young immigrant with photography in his blood. By the time he was fourteen, he was working as an assistant cameraman for Pathe News. When he was a photographer for the *Chicago Herald-American* in the 1920s, he took a freelance job shooting commercial aircraft at an aviation event at Chicago Municipal. Shortly afterward, taking photos at the airport would become his life's work for the next fifty years.

Rotunno not only photographed the famous stars, he even launched one star's career. In 1932, Dorothy Lamour, then a local girl with the Herbie Kay orchestra, came to the airport to sing Christmas carols. Rotunno poised Lamour next to an airplane, taking advantage of all of her attributes. When the shot ran in the paper the next day, it caused such a sensation that it propelled Ms. Lamour from singer to star.

In the era before non-stop transcontinental flights, Midway was the country's hub, requiring any celebrity traveling coast to coast to spend some time in Chicago. Whether it was Senator John F. Kennedy and wife Jackie arriving at midnight or Eleanor Roosevelt departing at 10 A.M., Rotunno was there on the tarmac, camera in hand.

Rotunno's photographs served two purposes: they gave the Hollywood Studios the attention they wanted for their stars, and they gave the airlines the attention they needed for themselves. For even during the 1940s and '50s, Americans were still afraid to fly. An image of a glamorous star showed that flying was as chic as traveling by Pullman sleeper car.

For example, if Elizabeth Taylor landed at Midway on TWA, Rotunno caught her deplaning on film, certain to include the TWA logo in the shot. If a newspaper published the photograph, Rotunno would be also collect a fee from the airline.

Rotunno had a knack for capturing the action of any situation. His photos' fluid sense of motion and movie-like feel became a personal trademark. And it didn't hurt that if a great photographic moment did not arise, Rotunno wasn't afraid to create one. He might arrange with the chef and staff of the Cloud Room to deliver a birthday cake to a star's table—candles ablaze and to the chorus of "Happy Birthday." Rotunno would get his photo of the baffled star, whose birthday could be six months away, and the star would get some cake.

After photographing a celebrity, Rotunno often invited them to dine at the Cloud Room. Rotunno recounted in a 1985 interview how he met Jimmy Stewart on a rainy day, took his picture, and then retired with him to the Cloud Room for some coffee. Due to the weather, Stewart had his hat pulled tight over his head. As Rotunno describes it, an excited waitress came up to their table: "'Mike, you know who's downstairs? It's Jack Benny.' I said, 'Well, take a look at Jimmy Stewart,' figuring she'd finally notice who it was. Instead she says, 'Ah, you can't make a fool out of me. That's just one of your crummy old newspaper pals,' and she walked off."[11]

According to Rotunno's daughter, Judy Anneaux, having a father in routine contact with the famous had certain advantages. It might mean taking a phone call at home from Jimmy Durante, letting Rotunno know that he'd be at Midway that evening. Or it meant having Duncan Renaldo, "The Cisco Kid," at your wedding. Mrs. Anneaux also remembers going with her father when he was called to the airport to meet the 7 A.M. flight of Harry S Truman (see p. 135). They joined the president who went straight to the Cloud Room and, being a tough Missourian, immediately ordered a shot of bourbon.

After fifty years of practicing his craft, Rotunno finally retired in 1980. He died in 1994, leaving behind many friends and admirers and an astonishing collection of photographs.

Today, celebrities jet from coast to coast in their private Gulfstream IVs and sip lattes at 35,000 feet. If they do land at Midway, their jet taxis to one of the Fixed Based Operators on the field, where they step out to waiting limos idling on the tarmac. The days of a star deplaning in the terminal with the rest of humanity are no more.

That era may be gone, but thanks to Mike Rotunno and his camera, it will not be forgotten.

Courtesy of the family of Mike Rotunno.

Left: Mike Rotunno, the legendary photographer and founder of Metro News. Anyone, from movie stars to presidents, got their picture snapped by Rotunno as they stepped off their plane at Midway Airport. Such P.R. created a positive image for airlines in an era when much of the public was still too skittish to fly.

Right: Mike Rotunno mugs for the camera with Phyllis Diller.

Photos by Mike Rotunno. Courtesy of the family of Mike Rotunno.

Left: John Wayne at Midway Airport. As was Rotunno's style, the TWA logo appears in the photograph. If the picture ran in the newspapers, TWA would pay Rotunno, a subtle form of merging star-power with advertising.

Right: Bud Abbott and Lou Costello deplane at Chicago Municipal Airport in 1946, and are met by Mike Rotunno's daughter Judy (left) and sister Mimi.

Former U.S. President Harry S Truman poses at Midway Airport with Mike Berry (left), Midway's general manager, and Mayor Richard J. Daley.

✈ Midway in the Movies

Despite the number of celebrities that passed through Midway Airport over the years, Arnie Bernstein's *Hollywood on Lake Michigan: 100 Years of Chicago and the Movies* (Lake Claremont Press, 1998) reveals that only a few movies have ever been made at Midway:

> Midway has been used in just a handful of films. In *Henry: Portrait of a Serial Killer* (1986), dimwitted Otis (Tom Towles) picks up his sister Becky (Tracy Arnold) here.
>
> Midway played a more pivotal role in Alfred Hitchcock's cross-country thriller, *North by Northwest* (1959). Having just been arrested for creating an art gallery disturbance, Roger Thornhill (the rakish Cary Grant) is brought to Midway by two Chicago cops. Shocked that he's being taken to the airport rather than jail, Grant demands some answers. He's quickly handed over to master agent Leo G. Carroll ("F.B.I. . . . C.I.A.. . . . O.N.I. . . .We're all in the same alphabet soup," he tells Grant), and the already twisted plot takes another sharp turn.
>
> Look closely during this scene and you'll notice two men in the background. Extras? Hardly. During the shoot, Bill Blaney, an airport worker at the time, and one of his colleagues sneaked onto the runway to sneak a peek at Cary Grant. Upon seeing the two men on the runway, Blaney recalled, Hitchcock was outraged. The master of suspense berated the duo for ruining his shot and ordered them to leave. Nevertheless, Blaney and his pal remained in the final cut, giving *North by Northwest* a slightly more realistic look, albeit through volunteer effort![12]

Left: James Stewart on the tarmac of Midway Airport, late 1940s. (Courtesy of Bill Aitken and David E. Kent.)

Right: Cary Grant listens to Alfred Hitchcock in the terminal of Midway Airport during the filming of *North by Northwest*. (Courtesy of Robert F. Soraparu. *Northwest Orient Airlines News* employee newsletter, Vol. 16, No. 1, Jan.–Feb. 1959.)

In the course of running his charter business, Pierce O'Carroll had the occasional strange experience. One woman hired him to fly over the lakefront. After takeoff, the woman began to sob uncontrollably. O'Carroll asked her what was the matter, and she explained that her husband had died. She then opened a box, took out an urn holding his ashes, slid back the canopy of the Ryan Navion, and pitched the ashes out of the cockpit. Unfortunately, due to the wind, most of the ashes blew back into the plane, and over O'Carroll, the lady, and the upholstery. After landing, O'Carroll stepped out of the plane to fetch a broom. Meanwhile, more customers took their seats in the plane for the next flight. When O'Carroll returned, the passengers were dusting ashes off their seats. "Careful," he said, "you never know who you might be sitting in!"

From the Lynch family collection.

The O'Carroll house, 3254 West Marquette Rd., on Chicago's South Side. Sheila O'Carroll often found it frustrating that her father could check up on whether she had done certain chores from his advantaged position in the air.

they weighed. He flew them in a Ryan Navion or the twin-engine Cessna, and before that in a Stinson or a Beechcraft. It was a twenty-minute ride over the Loop, Navy Pier, and the lakefront.

"So many people in Chicago can claim that their first ride was at the airport, and it was with my father or one of his pilots. My mother used to sell the tickets on Sundays in this little booth that we had, and she loved it and met very interesting people."

Lynch recollects fondly those Sundays at the airport: "It was fun. I remember it in my childhood. I can remember going out there in my First Communion dress and getting in trouble. I used to love to jump off the airplanes and I should have never been left in a dress—especially my First Communion dress, because of course it got hung up on the aileron; my First Communion dress was in shreds.

"There were also big numbers that were 50 feet long, numbers like '27 Left,' that identified the runways. Water would catch in these, and I remember floating boats in them and listening to the car radio before the battery would run down too far. I have very pleasant memories of Sundays out at the airport.

"Dad started out in a Jenny. Then he had a Curtiss and a variety of other planes. Later he had an AT-6, and then DC-3s and C-46s for the non-sked passenger flights.

"Once when I was ten, we went to pick up another Navion at the Ryan factory in California. Dad let me fly it all the way home. It took a couple of days because we'd land at night. And we had to go over the mountains. And it was 'Follow this railroad track,' or 'Keep the compass on this number,' as you would for a girl of ten at the time. I was thrilled."

✈

1. City of Chicago, *Journal of the Proceedings of the City Council*, 1949–50, 4423–4.

2. John A. Casey, *Chicago Aviation and Airports: The First Forty Years, 1926-1966* (Chicago Department of Aviation report, 1966), 17.

3. City of Chicago, Bureau of Parks, Recreation and Aviation, *Department of Public Works Annual Report*, 1951.

4. Robert M. Hill, *A Little Known Story of the Land Called Clearing* (Chicago: Chicago Historical Society, 1983), 222.

5. Casey, 20.

6. Stevenson Swanson, ed., *Chicago Days: 150 Defining Moments in the Life of a Great City* (Chicago: Contemporary Books, 1997), 181.

7. Hill, 210.

8. Ibid.

9. Tery Hunter, "Luxury, Excitement at the Cloud Room," *Chicago Sun-Times*, n.d. From the Marshall Field's archives.

10. "Cornfields to Crossroads," *Field Glass* 16 (Marshall Field's employee newsletter), 31 May 1949.

11. Jeff Lyons, "Imagemakers Heyday Relived in Flashbacks," *Chicago Tribune*, 20 June 1985.

12. Arnie Bernstein, *Hollywood on Lake Michigan: 100 Years of Chicago and the Movies* (Chicago: Lake Claremont Press, 1998), 261–2.

13. *Chicago Tribune* and *Chicago Daily News*, 13 July 1957.

14. Natty Dominique's Creole Dance Band, American Music (AMCD-18), liner notes (New Orleans: American Music Records).

15. Warren "Baby" Dodds, *The Baby Dodds Story, as told to Larry Gara* (Los Angeles: Contemporary Press, 1959), 95.

16. Eugene Cernan and Don Davis, *The Last Man on the Moon* (New York: St. Martin's Press, 1999), 29.

✈ July 12, 1957

Midway Airport became "Lake Midway" when Chicago received 6.24 inches of rain in a 24-hour period, the worst of the storm hitting between 7 P.M. Friday and 2 A.M. Saturday. Thousands of passengers were trapped in Midway's terminal as the water rose six inches inside the terminal, knocking out all phone and electricity service. Parts of the runways were covered in two feet of water, forcing the cancellation of all flights, while the parking lot was under four feet of water. Passengers slept on chairs, luggage, and even in grounded planes to keep dry. In an era before cell phones, five radio phones were brought in so passengers could call family members. Although it was a tense time, it was not without some levity. A passenger with a portable radio kept up the spirits of some stranded passengers, leading one couple to slosh through the water with a waltz. Roger Williams, a TWA employee, recounted how he and his colleagues walked past TWA Gate 14 dressed in rain gear, when a drunken passenger "stood up, came to attention and saluted us, and called out very loud, 'I salute you men of the submarine service!' Everyone within earshot roared."[13]

Courtesy of Bill Aitken and David E. Kent.

A boat floats on the tarmac at Midway Airport after a storm dumps 6.24 inches of water on the Chicago area, July 12, 1957.

✈ Redcap and Jazzman: Natty Dominique

One of the most remarkable characters on the Midway stage during the 1940s was Natty Dominique. Redcaps carried passengers' luggage through the terminal for tips; replete with stories and an engaging personality, Dominique was said to be the best of them. Perhaps that's because being a redcap was not his primary calling. Dominique was a famous jazz musician.

Anatole "Natty" Dominique was born in New Orleans in 1896, a Creole who had absorbed the emerging sound of his city: jazz. Dominique first trained as a drummer, but later switched to the cornet. He began his career with a New Orleans orchestra before moving to Chicago in 1913. Drawn to the South Side clubs, he played with Art Stewart and later with Jimmy Noone at the Paradise Café at 35th Street and Prairie Avenue. After a three year stint with the Carl Dickerson Orchestra, he moved to the Sunset Café at 35th Street and Calumet Avenue in the same band as fellow New Orleans cornetist Louis Armstrong. Over the years Dominique accompanied other jazz greats, including Jelly Roll Morton, who once made a recording playing a number of Dominique's original compositions.

Dominique's relationship with drummer Warren "Baby" Dodds would be the most significant. Baby Dodds and his older brother Johnny, a clarinetist, were both members of the legendary King Oliver's Creole Dance Band. With Louis Armstrong on cornet, they performed at the Lincoln Garden's Café on the South Side in the early 1920s. Dominique, the trained drummer, recognized Dodd's

Courtesy of Robert F. Soraparu.

The United Air Lines ticket area at Chicago Midway Airport, late 1950s.

talent, commenting that Baby was the best drummer he had ever heard.[14]

Natty played in bands until a heart condition sidelined his career, forcing him to seek work as a redcap at Chicago Municipal Airport in 1940, where he would find himself in the ironic position of carrying the luggage of musicians far less talented than himself. Dominique did not stray too long from his music, however, and in the 1950s formed Natty Dominique's Creole Dance Band. His band reached back to the early days of New Orleans jazz, celebrating the sounds of his youth. By 1951, drummer Baby Dodds had suffered two strokes; his drumming was affected by the strokes, but he still wanted to make music. Dominique invited him to play in his band. In Dodd's autobiography, he remembered that Natty's outfit ". . . was billed as one that played 'Slow Drag' music and that was because of me. I just couldn't beat drums fast, and to bring me into it Natty used to play lots of slow numbers. That way I could drum very well. Nobody but Natty Dominique would have done something like that."[15]

Dominique advised aspiring musicians to be original in their performance, and Natty Dominique was by all accounts an original jazz cat. It is a testament to his music that his recordings are still widely available fifty years later. Dominique's music could serve as the soundtrack of the airport's glory days, and if one listens to his recordings, the notes from his cornet fly as fast and as high as departing aircraft on takeoff.

THEY ALL LAND AT CHICAGO'S **MIDWAY AIRPORT**! ★ WITH BIGGEST TRAFFIC VOLUME IN U.S.A. © CURT TEICH & CO., INC. 3C-H563

From the author's collection.

As this postcard from the late 1950s shows, even alien visitors from Outer Space landed at Midway Airport.

✈ From Midway to the Moon

In the 1950s, when the DC-3 was still used for some passenger service, a young Purdue student from Bellwood, Illinois, took his first airplane ride on Lake Central Airlines, traveling from Midway Airport to West Lafayette, Indiana. The student's name was Eugene Cernan, whose first flight from Midway would lead to a more celestial landing decades later. Cernan went on to be the commander of Apollo XVII and was the last person to walk on the moon.[16]

✈ Midway's Top Cop: Tom O'Hara

Before there was an O'Hare in Chicago aviation, there was an O'Hara. Officer O'Hara. Thomas O'Hara's beat was Midway Airport from the mid-1930s until his retirement in 1955. Exiled to the airport early in his career for being too virtuous, O'Hara found himself both a lucky spectator of Midway's glory days and an important member of the Midway community.

An immigrant from Ireland, O'Hara was an honest cop in an age when corruption was reported in the ranks. He and his partner were plain-clothes officers "fond of knocking down cat houses," according to his son Jim, whereas the many cops on the take overlooked the houses of prostitution. O'Hara's targets included two brothels that apparently were "connected and protected." In fact, O'Hara had been specifically warned by his superiors to not interrupt their business. His father's response, Jim O'Hara recalls, was, "Too bad. What's right is right, and what's wrong is wrong." He raided the brothels and was immediately punished by his superiors with a transfer to a walking beat on the Southwest Side, which in the early 1930s was not much more than prairie.

O'Hara was not even in his new district three weeks before he discovered and broke up another brothel. His bosses immediately called him on it, decided he'd never learn, and "banished" him to the newly-built terminal of Chicago Municipal Airport where "he couldn't get into any trouble."

Far from the organized crime of the streets, O'Hara looked the other way to the petty hustling of a young airport entrepreneur, Louis Galina, and instead looked out for the hardworking and ambitious twelve-year-old. Galina had the first concession for a newspaper stand at Chicago's only airport. Besides selling newspapers to

individuals, Galina also supplied the airlines. When he realized that many passengers left their newspapers behind at the end of their flights, Galina gathered them up and resold them. Later in life, Galina worked for the railroads, became a police officer himself, and opened a restaurant on the Southwest Side.

At the terminal, the airport cops did not always have a great deal to do in the late 1930s, and a fondness for Galina did not preclude O'Hara and some of his fellow officers from having a little fun at his expense. Once the cops shaved off half the mustache the young Galina had such a hard time growing.

O'Hara's beat, however, was not just fun and games. There were gruesome aviation accidents, where O'Hara was often the first on the scene. In the era of propeller aircraft, a passenger would occasionally walk into a prop, especially on twin-engine aircraft. There were crashes off the field that needed to be attended to as well.

Still, Tom O'Hara's pleasant memories outnumbered the unpleasant ones, his family says. When American or foreign presidents, movie stars, and other celebrities landed at the airport, O'Hara had a front row view. One of the most memorable visits was that of Eamon DeValera, the former President of Ireland, who arrived at Midway Airport. On Midway's tarmac, O'Hara met the Irish president who, coincidentally, had been his classmate back in Ireland.

O'Hara lived to be 93, his quiet presence and sense of justice respected by those who had the pleasure of knowing him.

From a 2002 interview with James O'Hara.
Photo courtesy of James O'Hara.

Courtesy of Robert F. Soraparu.

Passengers wait in line at the United Air Lines ticket office in the terminal at Midway Airport, late 1950s.

A 1956
aerial view
of Midway's
terminal,
facing north,
with Cicero
Avenue
below.

✈ THE ASCENDANCY OF O'HARE AND THE BIRTH OF THE JET AGE

Phil Henderson. As a young man, Henderson led squadrons of B-26 bombers over German targets in World War II, flying 44 missions in all. Phil is one of the first Americans to see a jet, as a German jet got up close and personal with him as it tried to shoot down his bomber over Germany in the Spring of 1944. Henderson spent his professional life flying corporate jets out of Midway.

No single technological breakthrough in the twentieth century has done more to bring the world together than the jet engine. The agonizing flight of Lindbergh from New York to Paris that lasted 33 hours would in 30 years shrink to six hours. Although most people take jet technology for granted today, for Phil Henderson, a young bomber squadron leader flying missions over Germany during World War II, his first encounter with a jet would change his life.

"Returning to home base after dropping our bombs over Germany, our group was attacked by two ME-262s. The ME-262 is the first jet fighter in the world. They attacked the high flight, while I led the low flight. On his first pass, the jet fighter knocked out our number six plane, which descended into the clouds. I really don't know what happened to him; I'm sure they crashed. Our number three plane had about a foot knocked off the propeller. That put his engine out of balance and it was making gyrations. I thought it was going to tear itself off the airplane. He got the prop feathered, then he diverted to an alternate base. The ME-262 crossed from behind us to in front of us, turned around, and made a second pass. On the second pass, we drove him off without any further damage. That's my first experience with a jet.

"We were flying the fastest American bomber, the

A Lockheed L-1049 G flown by Lufthansa in front of the South Terminal (formally the first terminal) at Chicago Midway Airport, May 1956.

Courtesy of Robert F. Soraparu.

Drivers on Cicero Avenue in 1957 had a good view of the airplanes at Midway's terminal.

Passengers board a Chicago Helicopter Airways Sikorsky S-58C at Chicago Midway Airport, 1957.

Courtesy of Robert F. Soraparu.

A fueler tanks off a DC-6 at the American Airlines concourse, with the operations tower to the left, late 1950s.

B-26, and here's something that could go twice as fast. So there was a certain amount of envy. But they were on the other side, and we knew that eventually we'd have those.

"The creator of the jet engine was the guy who brought the world together. It is so commonplace now that people don't think anything about it, that you can be anywhere in the world from Chicago in twelve hours by jet airplane," Charles Downey noted. "Once, at American Airlines, a young lady complained to me, 'Mr. Downey, it took us seven hours to get to Greece on Olympic the other night!' I said, 'Young lady, it took me nine hours to get to Los Angeles once in a DC-6! Be happy that you have a jet airplane!'"

The post-war period, a time of great changes in American culture, was also a period of change for Midway, as planners began to look at the possibility of an international airport northwest of Chicago on the site of a small airfield known as Orchard Field.

"Jets were flying by the time O'Hare came along," David Young says. "Remember, O'Hare was planned in the '40s, right after World War II, and it didn't open until the late '50s. Actually, what became O'Hare was the old Douglas aircraft factory where they built military transport planes during World War II."

Phil Felper continues, "As for Midway, they figured there would never be jets—no, not here! Who would ever think of jets? So they doubled the size of the runway when they pulled the railroad tracks out and figured that's the biggest we'll ever need. All the land way down to Harlem Avenue belonged to the Board of Education, which is a long way, and it was all part of the airport. But the city said we don't need all that land.

"And the first thing you know, the jets started to fly. Now the field was too small. What are we going to do? The mayor [Richard J. Daley] said the only thing we can do is go up north and acquire some land from the suburbs. Which he did. He condemned all those little towns that were there. He closed cemeteries. And with that land he started adding on to the one runway that Orchard Field had. They fought him in court, but for the good of the public he eventually won out. So now, instead of going to a 5,000-foot runway at Midway, you could go to an 8,000- or 10,000-foot runway, which made a hell of a difference for jets."

And just as city leaders looked towards the great victory in the Pacific, the Battle of Midway, for inspiration to rename the South Side airport, they turned to World War II again when naming the newly-expanded Orchard Field. They named the airport in honor of Edward "Butch" O'Hare, a heroic naval fighter pilot.

"Butch O'Hare was an outstanding naval aviator," explains Charles Downey. "His father was from Chicago. I don't think Butch himself lived in the Chicago area, but he might have visited.

"He gained notoriety because he was an outstanding marksman. He flew a Wildcat fighter plane in combat and shot down five attacking twin-engine Betty bombers that were heading for his carrier. The

Courtesy of the City of Chicago, Department of Aviation.

Edward "Butch" O'Hare.

enemy had enough bombs aboard those five airplanes to sink the *Lexington*. It's remarkable that with the limited amount of ammunition he could shoot down five enemy aircraft in one short mission. He was probably only in the air an hour and a half and in actual combat about twenty minutes, destroying the attackers. This immediately placed him in line for a Congressional Medal of Honor.

"Butch O'Hare was one of the leaders who would have gone a long way up through naval hierarchy had he lived. During the war a plan was being developed for night-fighting capability. He was at the leading edge of that effort. He'd been in a Wildcat, but superior Hellcats were now in combat. Tactics were being worked out between the newer Grumman F6F Hellcat and an Avenger, which had a three-man crew, better radio equipment, and radar. The idea was to use the radar from the Avenger to lead the Hellcat fighter alongside to the enemy. From its exhaust flame pattern, O'Hare could then visually discern an enemy aircraft, line up, and shoot it down. In developing these tactics, he wound up missing on a mission one night. Conflicting stories exist that he ran into enemy firepower or friendly firepower. Whatever happened, we know we lost a great man."

With the advancement in technology, first with the introduction of four-engine aircraft and later the commercial jet aircraft, Midway Airport began to show its limitations. As jet technology was shrinking both time and distance, runways had to be longer. Midway with its limited size was seen as too small and calls for another airport went out. These appeals were

Courtesy of the City of Chicago, Department of Aviation.

Edward "Butch" O'Hare in the cockpit of his Grumman F-4F-3 Wildcat. In 1942, O'Hare shot down five Japanese bombers in one mission that were bound for the carrier *Lexington*. O'Hare was credited with saving the *Lexington*, for which he was awarded the Medal of Honor. He was lost over the Pacific in 1943, and the old Orchard Airport was renamed O'Hare Airport in his honor by the Chicago City Council in 1949.

The crowded South Terminal at Chicago Midway Airport in the 1950s, which served as the site of international boardings and departures.

Passengers deplane from a Mexicana DC-6 flight from Mexico City at the South Terminal at Midway Airport and prepare to enter Customs, January 5, 1960. According to Robert F. Soraparu, he was on the last Mexicana flight to leave Midway Airport for Mexico City on August 9, 1960. Coincidentally, Soraparu, was also on the first Mexicana flight to depart Midway Airport 42 years later, when international service was reintroduced at Midway in 2002.

A United Air Lines Mainliner Convair, parked on a wet tarmac at Chicago Midway Airport, 1953.

Left: Due to development in the region, by the 1950s Midway Airport was completely penned in, a victim of its own success. (From the Lynch family collection.)

Right: Two TWA Lockheed 1649 Jetstream Connies at the TWA hangar on 55th Street, 1961. The Eastern hangar is in the background. (Courtesy of Robert F. Soraparu.)

the beginning of O'Hare Airport.

Even after O'Hare officially opened in 1955, Midway was still the dominant Chicago airport and the busiest airport in the world. 1959 was its busiest year ever. But soon the initial trickle of business that moved north to O'Hare became a flood. The jets of that day, the 707s and DC-8s, needed longer runways and the improved O'Hare fit the bill.

However, as David Young states, "Even if the jet had not been developed as a feasible commercial aircraft, the enormous increase in size of propeller-driven aircraft such as the B-29 would have been a factor." Over time, all the four-engine ships went to O'Hare, and in the late 1960s, Midway became a ghost town. The busiest airport in the world became deadly quiet.

The drive for improvement fundamentally supposes that yesterday's invention will be replaced by tomorrow's technology. Just as the railway Pullman cars gave way to the DC-4s, so the piston aircraft gave way to the jet age. The early Municipal Airport, which in early photos appears lost in a field of grain, now fell victim—as Midway Airport "Crossroads of the World"—to its success. Homes and businesses had crowded around its borders, making the expansion of runways impractical.

"I was there at the time, in charge of moving the whole American Airlines operation to O'Hare," remembers Downey. "New terminals were built there to accommodate the Boeing 707. This was 1958 or 1959, which was the heyday of Midway as far as passenger traffic. We had coast-to-coast service at

Courtesy of Robert F. Soraparu.

A deserted United Air Lines gate at Midway Airport, 1960s.

✈ **1961**

Commercial flights at O'Hare surpass those at Midway Airport, and Midway relinquishes its title of "Worlds' Busiest Airport."[1]

✈ **March 23, 1963**

President John F. Kennedy rededicates O'Hare International Airport.

O'Hare." The American Airlines executives in New York City decided to move the whole American Airlines operation to O'Hare. Downey recalls what a

Two contrasts:

A tug pulls a DC-4 in front of the United Air Lines hangar on Cicero Avenue, late 1940s. (Courtesy of Robert F. Soraparu.)

Opposite: The same United hangar at Midway Airport, twenty years later, after being abandoned by United Air Lines in the 1960s. (Photo by Willy Schmidt, city photographer. Courtesy of the City of Chicago, Department of Aviation.)

✈ 1962

United Air Lines, the first airline to service Midway, is now the last to move its operations to O'Hare. W. A. Patterson, who had helped create the phenomenon that is today's United Airlines, says farewell to Midway, the proving ground of his airline. But as he leaves, Patterson makes a promise that United will one day return.

✈ July 13, 1962

The Chicago City Council passes a heliport licensing ordinance that it later amends on November 15, 1963.

✈ 1964

The Southwest Expressway, later renamed the Stevenson, is completed, reducing travel between the Loop and Midway from 45 to 30 minutes. Prior to this, the fastest way to Midway from downtown was along Archer Avenue.[2]

Mayor Richard J. Daley's efforts to revitalize the airport cause some carriers to return to Midway. A Boeing 727 is the first commercial jet to take off from Midway, witnessed by the mayor; William A. Patterson, CEO of United Air Lines; and hundreds of spectators. Although Midway will get some traffic, much is from cargo operations and Chicago Helicopter Airways, which this year increases its schedule to seven days a week and its flight service by 25 percent.[3]

Richard J. Daley had always appreciated the fact that Midway was close to downtown and understood the importance of Midway as an economic engine for the city. Daley, with the charisma and salesmanship that make him a political force locally and nationally, knows that to prevent the death of Midway, he needs to get the airlines interested in using the airport again. The airlines, content at O'Hare, want no part in moving back. The mayor, however, is able to convince some of them to put up token flights at Midway—just enough it seems—to keep the terminals from being totally vacant.

✈ December 31, 1965

Chicago Helicopter Airways ends operations.

✈ 1967–1968

The aging passenger terminal is rebuilt to handle DC-9s and 727s and the number of gates for aircraft is doubled to 28.[4] Before the redesign, aircraft parked parallel to the gates and passengers boarded outdoors from the ramp. With the new design, aircraft park perpendicular to the gates, customized so that a jet can power into the gate and be pulled by tug to exit. The depth of the terminal is also dramatically increased.

City officials figure that this new redesign will last for seven years. In reality, it lingers for over three decades. The outdated terminal is finally demolished and rebuilt as part of the Midway Terminal Development Program.[5]

✈ 1972

Several airlines reduce the number of daily flights in and out of the airport; operations at Midway begin to decrease.

✈ December 8, 1972

United Flight 533 from Washington D.C. ap-proaches Midway Airport and the tower radios the pilot to perform what is called a "missed approach" pattern. The pilot complies, yet 1.5 miles from the airport, the 737 hits the tops of the trees on 71st Street, before striking several bungalows and crashing into the home at 3722 70th Place. The occupants, Mrs. Veronica Kuculich and her daughter Theresa, are killed. A total of 45 people are killed in the crash, 43 in the plane, including the three-person crew, and two on the ground. Eighteen passengers survive.

The crash garners national headlines due to the fact that one of the passengers, Mrs. Dorothy Hunt, is the wife of E. Howard Hunt, one of the Watergate conspirators indicted for breaking into the Democratic National Committee Headquarters. Mrs. Hunt's recovered purse contains $10,585 in cash. There is speculation in the press about a link between this money and a Nixon slush fund, with a rumor of sabotage as well. After an investigation by the National Transportation Safety Board, however, pilot error is cited as the cause of the crash: the crew became distracted after the tower told them to abort their approach and, having not deactivated the jet's spoilers, stalled and crashed.[6]

✈ 1973

The oil embargo and fuel shortages hit commercial aviation along with the rest of the nation. All the major carriers return to O'Hare, and Midway is once again a ghost town.

Still, flight students and corporations with private aircraft rediscover Midway during this period. Pilots appreciate the lack of a waiting time and the airport's proximity to downtown Chicago.

Midway-- A Deserted Ghost Field

Business Went to O'Hare Along with the Airlines

BY ED KANDLIK

Chicago's Midway Airport, once the world's busiest, has become the center of a disaster area.

Had they been struck by an earthquake or a plague, some of the business people there would hardly be worse off. In the airport terminal you could bowl in the halls with no danger of hitting anybody.

Only 13 commercial flights a day are scheduled from Midway. Eight are on United, to such points as Washington, Cleveland and Detroit; two on Braniff, and three on Delta, including one all-cargo flight. In 1959 scheduled commercial flights from Midway reached a peak of about 1,300 daily.

The last mass migration of planes and personnel from Midway to O'Hare Airport was on April 29.

Eastern Air Lines, Lake Central Airlines and Ozark Air Lines facilities are closed. At TWA attendants were even moving out the furniture.

* * *

MAYOR Daley has asked

Pictures on Back Page

the Civil Aeronautics Board to stop the last of the lines from leaving.

The depression at Midway was deepened by United Air Lines' removal of its headquarters and 1,300 employes Dec. 8, 1961 to northwest of the city.

The thousands of passengers who used to crowd the airport's lobbies, are no longer there, nor are the airline pilots, stewardesses, and ground personnel.

"I'm glad I'm getting out of here," a discouraged porter

Turn to Page 12, Column 3

Above: An agent carries away a ticket counter sign, while the last United flight to depart Midway Airport stands in the background, July 9, 1962. United Air Lines was the last carrier to move its operations to O'Hare Airport. (Courtesy of Robert F. Soraparu.)

Right: A newspaper headline states how bleak it had become at Midway during the lean years after the airlines left. By 1963, Midway was all but abandoned. (Courtesy of Marshall Field's.)

From the Lynch family collection.

Left: Pierce "Scotty" O'Carroll, whose career at Midway traced the evolution of the airport over four decades, ironically died when the field was dying.

Right: Pierce O'Carroll obituary, 1961.

Pioneer Pilot O'Carroll Dies In New York

Pierce (Scotty) O'Carroll, 62, a pioneer Chicago pilot who operated the Monarch Air Service at Midway Airport since 1929, died of a stroke Saturday in French Hospital, New York City.

PIERCE O'CARROLL

Mr. O'Carroll, of 3254 W. Marquette Rd., was a native of County Leix, Ireland. He came to Chicago in 1924 and learned flying while employed as a bus driver.

He founded Monarch with a partner but split the partnership when he found a training plane for sale cheap in 1931. His erstwhile partner hired a man for $50 to pose as a pupil and sabotage O'Carroll's plane. The hireling caused the plane to crash, knocking out O'Carroll's teeth.

Besides teaching flying, Mr. O'Carroll flew charter flights. Four years ago, he had another stroke and had to give up flying. Since then, his firm has been engaged in fueling non-scheduled airline flights.

Survivors include the widow, Rose; a daughter, Shiela; three sisters and four brothers in England, Ireland, and Australia.

Requiem mass will be offered at 10:30 a.m. Tuesday in St. Nicholas of Tolentine Church. Burial will be in Holy Sepulchre Cemetery.

The body is in the James E. Egan Funeral Home, 3700 W. 63d.

✈ On a personal note, the O'Carroll family would experience a loss at the same time that Midway was dying. Pierce "Scotty" O'Carroll was young when the airport was young; he had made his life at the airport and saw it change over forty years. This pilot, who had spent thousands of hours in the air during aviation's most dangerous days, died on the ground. In 1961, O'Carroll suffered a fatal stroke in New York City. The plane carrying his casket back to Chicago landed in the dark; the tower had dimmed the runway lights for the pilot's final landing at Midway Airport.

difficult relocation that was for Midway employees: "A lot of airport people living around Midway just did not want to move. They found it a hardship. It was tough for them.

"The move was delayed twice. I had all these trucks all lined up, and I said, 'We're going to move this weekend. We're paying a penalty with all these trucks standing by.' People were instructed to come to work at O'Hare Field on Monday. I set up a bus service from an employee parking lot, the old Air Force facility at O'Hare on Mannheim Road. We didn't have a lot of people at the time, not like you have today. It was enough. I think we eventually moved about 1,100 people up there from Midway in 1960–61. We left a token freight service at Midway and kind of locked things down. It was really a skeleton of its former status."

"When the airlines left, it killed the airport and the neighboring businesses. All the hotels, motels, and restaurants were closing." [PF]

Downey says about that depressed time, "You didn't have guys going to the barber shop down the street, eating at the delis, or using the banks who had their accounts. I was there at the time; I had an office in both places for over a year because I was in charge of financial activities for the airline in Chicago."

Yet over the same period, hotels and motels were springing up near O'Hare. Downey adds, "United Air Lines reluctantly moved. They hired a bus service to bring people who reported to Midway to O'Hare and then drove them home at the end of the day. They wanted to keep their key employees."

The airport that rose from the onion field in 1926 was dying. For those who loved Midway and saw it develop into the busiest airport in the world, its decline was indeed heartbreaking.

✈

1. Stevenson Swanson, ed., *Chicago Days: 150 Defining Moments in the Life of a Great City* (Chicago: Contemporary Books, 1997), 181.

2. John A. Casey, *Chicago Aviation and Airports: The First Forty Years, 1926-1966* (Chicago Department of Aviation report, 1966), 32.

3. Ibid.

4. City of Chicago, Department of Aviation, *Annual Report*, 1967.

5. Conversation with Paul Shaver, project architect for the 1967–68 Midway terminal redesign, 19 September 2001.

6. Ellen O'Brien and Lyle Benedict, "1972, December 8; Crash of United Airlines Flight 533," http://www.chipublib.org/0004chicago/disasters/flight533_crash.html, accessed 17 September 2001.

A Delta Convair 880 and a TWA L-1049 Super "G" Constellation at O'Hare International Airport, 1963.

Part IV

Cleared for Takeoff
1964–2001

✈

Photo by Peter J. Schulz, city photographer. Courtesy of the City of Chicago, Department of Aviation.

Sunlight floods in through large windows, illuminating the interior of the new Midway terminal, 2001.

✈ Stall, Spin, and Recovery

ven as the airlines began to abandon Midway for the larger runways of O'Hare, Midway had a strong ally on the fifth floor of City Hall.

Charles Downey remembers: "Never did Mayor Richard J. Daley think there wouldn't be a Midway Airport. It was being kept alive by the force of his personality. He was adamant about the airlines maintaining some service there. The tradeoff was that American and the other carriers would come back if they had newer terminal facilities. When they left, the terminal was primitive, not even up to small jet standards.

"That was done, and the carriers came back. They diligently put in schedules that would connect to each other. It proved to be disastrous. American lost $11 million the first year; Delta lost $6 million, as did United; all in a valiant effort to respond to the mayor's wishes. The economics just weren't there for the trunk carriers to come to Midway and create a duplicate of what they had at O'Hare. As a result,

they pulled away, only Delta remaining to the end."

"Small aircraft were the only things that kept Midway viable," comments Thomas Goldthorpe. "It was virtually abandoned. There were weeds growing up in the seams of the concrete on the runways.

Above: Mayor Richard J. Daley and W. A. Patterson, the Chairman and CEO of United Air Lines. The Mayor was Midway's strongest advocate during its lean years, convincing the skeptical airlines to maintain some flights at Midway. (Courtesy of the City of Chicago, Department of Aviation.)

Left: Mayor Richard J. Daley and W. A. Patterson stand on the platform at inaugural ceremonies for the resumption of service by United Air Lines at Chicago Midway Airport, July 5, 1964. (Courtesy of Robert F. Soraparu.)

Left: A Sikorsky S-58 parked at Midway Airport in 1971. Helicopter service came back to the airport briefly in the 1970s, but soon faded.

Above, left: A Boeing 727 on the tarmac of Chicago Midway Airport, one of the first scheduled flights that United Air Lines introduced in 1964. United's service to New York's La Guardia Airport was the first commercial jet service from Midway.

Above, right: Two Air Mid-America Convair 600s at Chicago Midway Airport, early 1970s.

Courtesy of Robert F. Soraparu.

There was no parking provided for small aircraft. If you wanted to park your airplane at Midway Airport, you created a parking space by laying down steel matting over the mud so your airplane wouldn't sink up to its axles. You installed your own tie-downs. There was no organization, no planning by the city. To top this, the owners were charged $30 a month by the city for the privilege of improving their land."

In the early 1970s, while O'Hare grew louder with jet noise and its air traffic became congested, the runways and terminals of Midway were empty and quiet.

David Young recalls visiting Midway's vacant terminal during this bleak time in the airport's history: "I remember coming in here when it was dead in the early '70s. I mean, you could throw hand grenades in the lobby and not kill anybody. You might wake a sleeping janitor."

And airport security, such a critical component to airports today, was quite lax. Tom Goldthorpe's story demonstrates just how casual it was: "One of my former students bought a new Corvette and he was allowed to see how fast it would go down one of the active runways, because he had a friend who worked in the control tower. And he went out there in the wee hours of the morning and got his Corvette up to about 130 miles an hour while going down runway 22 Left."

Ironically, the dead silence over Midway's runways would become its greatest asset, and corporate America began to take notice.

The reality was that Midway had been losing its esteem. The old-timers were heartsick at leaving, yet once scrappy young pilots like Phil Felper, who flew the old Jennys in the 1930s at Midway, were now the captains of the sleek jets. They had to go where the jets were going. But they went reluctantly.

Eventually all of the major airlines left Midway. W. A. "Pat" Patterson, who had helped create the phenomenon that is today's United Airlines, said farewell to Midway, the proving ground of his airline. As he left, however, Patterson made a promise that United would one day return.

"The business people ate it up because they could come into Midway and be downtown in nothing

Forty years after the DC-3 first made its appearance on the airfield, Air Mid America brought DC-3 service back to Midway Airport in the 1970s. This small carrier operated for a short time at the airport.

Courtesy of Robert F. Soraparu.

Although passengers still boarded aircraft from the tarmac with the 1967–68 terminal redesign, the use of jetways was anticipated and the gates were engineered to accommodate that form of loading when it was brought to Midway fifteen years later.[1]

Prior to the late 1960s, passengers' luggage at Midway was brought from the tarmac and usually loaded onto an outdoor slide covered from the elements. With the redesign, baggage was moved indoors, a novel approach during that era, and a concept taken for granted by today's travelers.[2]

Courtesy of Robert F. Soraparu.

An aerial view facing southwest of the terminal and Runway 22L, early 1970s.

flat," said corporate pilot Felper. "And that's the same time Merrill Meigs put his field up, Meigs Field. He used to come in here with his airplane.

"Gradually I brought my jets in here because my costs of operation went way down. I didn't have to wait in line to be number twenty for takeoff. I could get off right away. And when I needed spare parts, I could get them all here overnight. Why did I want to be someplace where I'd spend five times as much money for operating? Many of the other businesspeople started feeling the same way—Standard Oil, Sears Roebuck, and others. Why did we want to be at O'Hare with such a rough time getting in and out during the rush part of the day after a two-hour wait? It would ruin your schedules."

As corporations moved their air fleets to Midway from O'Hare, some of the airlines began to notice that Midway's lack of traffic could be an attractive alternative to the gridlock at O'Hare.

"What did that was deregulation and the arrival of the low-cost carriers," says David Young. "Suddenly the low-cost carriers couldn't get slots at O'Hare, and if they could, it was much more expensive than at Midway. It made all the sense in the world to come to Midway. The first one was Midway Airlines."

"I was their key man in Chicago," adds Charles Downey. "We set up a small office on 55th Street. We would receive tons of applicants in the mail. The economy was depressed so it was a big gamble because money had to be raised. We started Midway Airlines with $3½ million and three borrowed DC-9 planes. We nearly closed three months after opening.

Courtesy of Robert F. Soraparu.

We needed to get another $3 million to stay alive.

"Then it took off and worked for a time. Some management mistakes were made in its ten-year history and it hit a financial obstacle. But the idea that a newcomer has to come in with a favorable fare differential is still a good one because there's always a part of the marketplace that will respond to a lower price.

"Much is happening that makes it a very viable airport, and it will continue to be whether or not a third airport comes into being. If you look at the Los Angeles basin, you see several large airline airports. An airline with the freedom to operate a carrier that knows what it's doing will seize the opportunity at a

A Midway Metrolink DC-9 parked at Chicago Midway Airport during the mid-1980s. The Metrolink experiment handled business class service for the entire fleet. The carrier changed its name back to Midway Airlines, however, after the concept did not take off with the public.

Photo by Willy Schmidt, city photographer. Courtesy of the City of Chicago, Department of Aviation.

A Midway Airlines DC-9 takes off at Chicago's Midway Airport. Midway Airlines began with three jets in 1979, and with its growing success, showed that Midway Airport could again become a viable airport for commercial passenger traffic.

Above, left: Several Midway Metrolink DC-9s parked at Midway in the mid-1980s. (Courtesy of Robert F. Soraparu.)

Above, right: Passengers arrive and depart from Midway Airport's terminal as the airport revives in the late 1980s. (Photo by Willy Schmidt, city photographer. Courtesy of the City of Chicago, Department of Aviation.)

Right: A Gulfstream III, owned by Square D and piloted by Philip Felper, mid-1980s. Square D, like many other companies, kept their corporate jets at Midway Airport, where they enjoyed the benefits of no traffic or delays in departures or arrivals. (Courtesy of Philip Felper.)

✈ 1977

Air traffic increases slightly and efforts are made to use Midway as a low-fare commuter airport.

✈ 1979

Midway Airlines is formed and provides flights to Kansas City, Detroit, and Cleveland.

✈ 1980

Northwest Airlines returns to Midway, with flights to Minneapolis.

✈ February 28, 1982

The City of Chicago purchases Midway Airport from the Board of Education for $16 million.

✈ 1985

Southwest Airlines, a former intrastate carrier from Texas, begins service to Midway Airport.[3]

✈ 1987

The City of Chicago celebrates Midway's sixtieth anniversary.

✈ March 25, 1991

Midway Airlines declares bankruptcy and 4,000 jobs are lost in the area, proving how important an economic vehicle the airport is for the city.[4]

✈ 1992

American Trans Air (ATA) opens a hub at Chicago Midway Airport.[5]

✈ 1993

The Chicago Transit Authority and the City of Chicago finish construction of the Orange Line, an extension of the rapid transit system that makes Midway accessible from downtown and most other areas of the city. The CTA had been running trains to O'Hare since 1984.

✈ 1995

Southwest Airlines signs a major contract with the City of Chicago, which will ensure its place as a significant force in the Midway of the future.

✈ 1997

The city announces the Midway Terminal Development Program to redesign the airport's aging terminal. This ambitious $761-million project becomes the largest public works program in Illinois. One of the first tasks is to reroute South Cicero Avenue 2,300 feet eastward.[6]

✈ 1998

Midway serves 11.4 million passengers, making it the fasting growing airport in North America.[7]

✈ 1999

A 3,000-car parking garage opens at Midway, offering covered parking for the first time in its history, a real advantage in the snowy winter months.[8]

✈ 2001

Southwest has 121 daily flights to Chicago, or 108,529 seats available weekly.[9]

✈ March 7, 2001

Midway's state of the art, multi-million dollar, 900,000-square-foot terminal is dedicated as part of the Midway Airport Terminal Development Program (MATD).[10] Midway's remarkable evolution is also due in part to substantial commitments from Southwest Airlines and ATA, two carriers who realize Midway's potential. The renovation will be completed in 2004, and the number of gates will increase from 29 to 41.[11]

✈ May 10, 2001

Boeing, the giant aerospace company, announces that it is relocating its headquarters from Seattle to Chicago. Boeing officials fly to Midway Airport where they are met by Chicago mayor Richard M. Daley and Illinois governor George H. Ryan. The fact that Boeing lands at Midway is entirely appropriate in that the first commercial flight to the airport in 1927 was for Boeing Air Transport.[12]

Mayor Daley announces a $98-million pilot training center to be located at the Midway Gateway Center at Cicero and Archer Avenues. The center will have a flight simulator for pilots, as well as training facilities for flight attendants and mechanics.[13]

✈ September 11, 2001

The cataclysmic attack and destruction of the World Trade Center towers in Manhattan and the Pentagon in Washington D.C. cause the Federal Aviation Administration to ground all air traffic in the United States. The next day, the skies over Midway remain silent; for the first time in 75 years, there are no takeoffs or landings. Airport officials at Midway, and all airports in the United States, must struggle with the reality of terrorism while balancing the demand for security with the freedoms inherent in an open society.

place like Burbank today, which is coming alive. There's John Wayne Airport that was the old Orange County Airport. Chicago has parallels to the Los Angeles basin. You've got Milwaukee Airport nearby for North Siders. People are always going to come to where there's good value and convenience. Midway Airport is convenient."

Sheila Lynch: "Midway had very lean times in the 1960s when it looked like it was going to shut down, and in the '90s when there was talk about a third airport shutting down Midway. But Midway has survived. It's very important to have an in-town airport. Meigs Field is fine, but it's not big enough and there are problems with bad weather.

"O'Hare is tremendous in size and extremely busy, making Midway very convenient for corporate aircraft as well as passengers to use. It's easy to fly in and out as well as to drive in and out."

"The airlines," Dave Young mentions, "rediscovered the older airports. Southwest Airlines, the big operator at Midway, stayed with Love Field in Dallas long after the big airlines abandoned it."

As politicians, airlines, noise abatement groups, and others debate the merits of a third airport, it's easy to lose sight of how an airport like Midway came about—through individual efforts and the courage of those early aviation pioneers who cherished their ability to fly like eagles.

The story of flight is as much the story of the heroes who fought to make aviation respected as they led America and the world into a new era. Progress in

From the Lynch family collection.

Monarch Air Service's general manager, Mike Crosse; Fred Farbin; and Monarch's president, Matthew J. Lynch celebrate Farbin's forty years of employment at Midway Airport, 1984.

flying may be the result of technological advances, but it took the men and women who flew these machines to make the dream come true. Scotty O'Carroll respected these legends of flight and was thrilled when his flying business received a visit from the ultimate aviation icon.

According to Sheila Lynch, "A private aircraft came in piloted by a woman, with an older man as a passenger who was handling the payment for the fuel. Fred Farbin, who was just a teenager at the time, serviced the aircraft and presented the man with the invoice." As Farbin described it, the procedure was to put the customer's name and address on the invoice, regardless if it was cash or charge: "So I asked this

Photo by Willy Schmidt, city photographer. Courtesy of the City of Chicago, Department of Aviation.

Mayor Harold Washington admires a jet in the newly dedicated hangar for Midcon-Natural Gas Pipeline Co. of America, at Midway Airport, October 31, 1986. Midcon's chief pilot, Dave Stubbs, is to the mayor's right.

older gentleman for his name, and he said, 'Orville Wright,' and I started writing 'Orville' and I thought to myself, 'Who's this joker?' I turned around, and then I recognized him.

"Just then Tony Mackiewicz, one of our pilots at the time, came out. Orville had signed a special racing license for Tony some years before, a race from Chicago to Seattle.

"We were all shooting the breeze out there and Orville was getting ready to go when Scotty pulled up in his car. He said, 'Wasn't that Orville Wright?' and I said, 'Yeah, that was him,' and Scotty said, 'Is his signature on the bill?' And I said, 'No . . . cash sale.' Of course Scotty got mad as hell!"

Sheila Lynch elaborates, "Well, Dad was so upset, 'What do you mean you didn't give him free gasoline!' And Dad never let him forget it."

With a twinkle in his eye, Fred wryly stated, "But my orders were if it was a cash sale, just put the name and address down for the tax refund, and no signature required."

✈   ✈   ✈

Author: "Do we have any more heroes like Lindbergh and Doolittle?"

Charles Downey: "Yes, but they are of a different kind. You can find them."

Author: "Why does aviation have such giants?"

Downey: "Because flying is so dramatic. Not too many people do it. There are only 600,000 pilots in the United States. There are only a handful of airline pilots. And just a few astronauts. Flying is still an adventurous thing at the leading edge. We're talking about space travel now. We're talking about some Russians who have logged 400-plus days in space."

Author: "Space is the new frontier."

Downey: "It's *the* frontier. Supersonic is no big deal."

Thomas Goldthorpe: "Probably more people know the name of Charles Lindbergh than know the name of Neil Armstrong. Armstrong was part of a gigantic team. Lindbergh pretty much accomplished what he did through his own efforts."

Author: "Do you think our new Lindbergh will be in space?"

Downey: "I think all the Lindberghs are in space now."

Goldthorpe: "Maybe there will be heroes in the future, space heroes. The first to go to Mars or Venus or whatever. But it is not going to be an individual effort. No more Lone Eagles. No more Jimmy Doolittles leading his men on a raid over Tokyo. No more bicycle mechanics [the Wright Brothers] who dream of flying in the face of ridicule. Eminent scientists like Samuel Langley weren't able to achieve what a couple of bicycle mechanics who didn't have a high school diploma between them were able to achieve. The world has changed. It's a little sad."

✈   ✈   ✈

A Midway Airlines jet and Southwest Airlines aircraft share the ramp at Chicago Midway Airport, late 1980s. Once Midway Airlines proved that passenger traffic could be profitable at Midway Airport, other carriers came to Midway Airport, including Southwest Airlines, which arrived in 1985. Other low cost carriers, like ATA, would also begin service at Midway.

EVEN THOUGH SEVERAL decades have passed since this farmer's field became an airport, one aspect of Midway seems to never change. There are still individuals of all ages who pause for a moment when they hear a jet thunder on its takeoff roll and stare in wonder as it rises overhead, wishing they could be aboard. And even pilots like Phil Felper, who has logged thousands of hours of flight time, still get excited talking about flying. For Felper, flying brought freedom and the chance to travel the world.

"When I graduated from junior high someone had written in my yearbook: 'Phil Felper, a pilot will be, will cross the briny sea.' I'll never forget that. I thought I had no chance of doing that. I'd never cross the briny sea. But the people in the class had that down. And I'll be damned if that didn't happen. I crossed the Pacific, the Atlantic, I crossed all over the world, Australia, everywhere."

When Fred Farbin sat for an interview in 1985, shortly before his death, he reminisced and marveled at the acceleration of aviation technology he had personally witnessed in his lifetime. When Farbin saw a DC-3 for the first time, he exclaimed, "My God, they can't get any bigger." To Fred, aviation always meant change.

"And look what we've seen," he mused. "And it wouldn't surprise me that what you see right now [jets] will be total junk in forty years."

Fred's last statements to the author were not nostalgic stories of the airport's past, but a vision of Midway's future. Without any hint of sarcasm, Fred stated matter-of-factly that this former onion field will one day not be a place of jets, but of rockets blasting on to their celestial destinations.

✈

Photo by Peter J. Schulz, city photographer. Courtesy of the City of Chicago, Department of Aviation.

Mayor Richard M. Daley is greeted by enthusiastic Southwest Airlines employees wearing orange on the 1993 dedication of the Chicago Transit Authority's Orange Line that links Chicago's Loop with Midway Airport.

Photo by Peter J. Schulz, city photographer. Courtesy of the City of Chicago, Department of Aviation.

The new arrival area at Midway Airport, one of the major improvements as part of the Midway Airport Terminal Development Program.

Photo by Peter J. Schulz, city photographer. Courtesy of the City of Chicago, Department of Aviation.

The interior of the new Midway terminal ticketing area that opened on March 7, 2001, as part of the Midway Airport Terminal Development Program.

1. Conversation with Paul Shaver, project architect for the 1967–68 terminal redesign, 19 September 2001. Since Chicago's first official airport received its first terminal seventy years ago, the terminal has been redesigned four times in 1931, 1947, 1968, and 2001.

2. Conversation with Paul Shaver, project architect for the 1967–68 terminal redesign, 19 September 2001.

3. Southwest Airlines Web site, www.southwest.com, accessed 9 August 2001.

4. *Chicago Sun-Times*, 13 October 1991.

5. American Trans Air Web site, www.ata.com, accessed 12 August 2001.

6. This was not the first time in Midway's history that a transportation right-of-way was moved because of airport expansion. As noted previously, the Chicago Belt Railway tracks that ran along 59th Street were rerouted in 1941 to allow for longer runways.

7. "Chicago's Midway Airport: A Historic Redevelopment," *Chicago Sun Times*, 15 July 2001.

8. Ibid.

9. Southwest Airlines Web site, www.southwest.com, accessed 9 August 2001.

10. City of Chicago, Office of the Mayor, press release, 9 April 2001.

11. "Chicago's Midway Airport: A Historic Redevelopment," *Chicago Sun Times*, 15 July 2001.

12. City of Chicago, Office of the Mayor, press release, 10 May 2001.

13. City of Chicago, Office of the Mayor, press release, 7 March 2001.

Epilogue:

A Monarch Farewell

✈

The massive doors of Monarch's hangar at night.

✈ Epilogue:
A Monarch Farewell

It was 10 P.M. on the warm night of June 4, 1997. I was the last to arrive, as my sister Katie and brother Brendan waited for me in the parking lot next to Monarch's hangar. I had been delayed buying the champagne at a store along the way to Midway Airport. I got out of the car and greeted them as they milled around Monarch's entrance, hesitant it seemed to go inside.

I certainly shared their sentiment, for after 65 years Monarch Air Service was now just hours away from being sold to a multinational corporation. We were here, not to bear witness to the turning over of a company, but rather to say good-bye.

I heard a muffled sound in the sky, looked up, and saw an object floating in the darkness just a few hundred yards away, pointing right at me, its gigantic shape illuminated. It was the sort of sight that made one catch one's breath. Although I knew it was the Goodyear blimp, in town for game three of the NBA finals between the Chicago Bulls and the Utah Jazz, it still was a shock, for it did indeed look like a UFO from another world.

The blimp buzzed directly overhead, then nose-dived in front of the hangar where the grounds crew caught its dangling ropes and pulled it down to the tarmac—an operation that echoed bygone days when lighter-than-air ships were as plentiful as commercial airliners. Witnessing such a simple procedure at Midway seemed appropriate, since Midway's roots reached back to the dawn of human flight.

Monarch had always been a Ma and Pa operation, dating back to the 1930s when flying was still a novelty and anyone with a plane could potentially become an airline. But as aviation changed and became more corporate, the Ma and Pa businesses began to disappear. Although Monarch thrived during these decades and outlasted most in the field, the time had finally come to call a code blue. Tonight was the last hours of its existence.

We entered the hangar through doors covered by

Courtesy of Harold Lind.

Midway Airport at night, when its thousands of blue and white electric bulbs bathe the field in magnificent light.

a green canopy, Monarch's color. I couldn't help but notice that the name "Monarch" had been covered over. The new owners had wasted no time.

In the brightly-lit lounge area, the usual assortment of pilots and passengers were sitting on couches and chairs watching the basketball game. Red, a Monarch employee for many years, was behind the counter, having just arrived for his night shift. He wore a new white shirt with the name of the new owner stitched on the breast pocket. I shook Red's hand, "You look better in green, Red." We both laughed.

As my sister and brother's attention was drawn to the TV, I walked behind the counter and poured myself a cup of good old Monarch coffee. It didn't matter, day or night, there was always hot coffee at Monarch, free to anyone in the hangar. To pilots, coffee was almost as important as jet fuel.

I sipped my coffee out of a Styrofoam cup and leaned over the counter, talking with Red about the old times. Red had worked the night shift as long as anyone could remember, and I always envied his job, for it was at night that Midway's splendor was visible. In the sunshine, one could see the cracks in the tarmac with the occasional weed sprouting up, but as darkness descended, the airport was transformed into something wonderful, an ocean of lights shimmering on a black canvas. The blue lights along the runways would twinkle in the night air, and the sight of it would take your breath away.

For Red, nights meant working alone or with an assistant, a shift that had no telephones ringing or a lot of nosy questions or customer complaints. Nights also meant that Red met everyone. Bill Cosby was a regular visitor. Flying in on his private jet, Cosby would often call Red from the air to make arrangements for catering or limos or whatever the entertainer might need. There was one late night when Cosby stayed inside the lounge watching the remaining moments of a ball game while his annoyed wife sat in a limo outside, waiting.

Perhaps the best Red anecdote was about one night when he was working at the old hangar next to the current one. Mike Crosse, Monarch's general manager, had distributed a memo that day stressing the need to curb the expensive long distance phone calls that pilots were making. Red was ready to enforce the new policy.

A man walked up to the small, high counter. Sitting behind it, Red could not clearly see who was on the other side. The visitor asked Red if he could use Monarch's phone. Thinking it was a freight pilot, notorious mooches, Red growled, "Use the pay phone like everyone else!" The man quickly retreated.

Red never lived down his embarrassment when he found out that the man at whom he had barked was George Herbert Walker Bush, the Vice President of the United States.

It was time for my brother, sister, and I to take our final hangar walk-around. I led the way through a set of doors. Corporate aviation, the mainstay of Monarch's business, is a behind-the-scenes enterprise most Americans do not know exists. It is an indicator of the so-called good life that only a privileged few,

Courtesy of Harold Lind.

Sleek corporate jets stacked inside Monarch's main hangar.

ately known as "Lake Sheila" after my mother. The masonry bestowed upon the hangar a kind of elegance that masked its bulky exterior. The fluorescent lights on the ceiling reflected off the shiny jets below and gave the hangar an ethereal radiance at night.

Architect Paul Shaver added little touches to the box-shaped building. Where the three-story office building met the hangar, the bulk of the hangar's roof climbed higher, and to take advantage of the overlap, Shaver put in a clerestory (a disconnected expanse just under the roof) to allow natural sunlight to flood the interior from windows that ran the width of the hangar. This same principle illuminates French gothic cathedrals with the glow of stained glass. Shaver's inspiration came from a town hall in Norway, proving that a good architectural motif can enhance any structure, even an airplane hangar.

The annual Monarch Christmas party was always held in the hangar. Holiday cheer abounded for the crowd, thanks in part to the free drinks. It was fun to circulate among the sleek jets and greet colleagues and friends. If things got rowdy, or if the party was running late, there was one sure way of bringing it to an end. The great twin doors of the hangar would be opened and a blast of frigid December air would freeze the celebrants. One evening, I heard a radio interview with Bob Hope during which the host reminisced about first meeting the comedian when his plane landed at Midway and was towed into a hangar during a party. As Hope disembarked, a band began to play and everyone danced.

Our tour ended. We still needed to have a cham-

the ones who ride in these private jets, enjoy. As always, I was stunned by the sheer size of the cavernous hangar. Though I had seen it a thousand times I was always surprised by the enormity of the space. It was big enough to stack several corporate jets behind the creaking gigantic doors. Imagine the side of a warehouse shaking before rising as huge counterweights pulled the doors upward.

The massive hangar was built with steel girders and masonry in the early 1980s when my father, Matthew Lynch, realized that to stay competitive in corporate aviation his facilities needed upgrading. Due to excavation work, water collected where the hangar's floor would go, and this pool was affection-

pagne toast before the hour of midnight when owner-ship would be transferred. I retrieved the bottle of bubbly I had bought earlier. It slipped out of my hand and smashed on the tarmac. A more fitting tribute to Monarch, I thought, like the christening a ship. But now we had only 20 minutes to find something else to fill our glasses.

My brother said, "There's still something we have to see," and motioned towards the old hangar, dark except for the red roof lights signaling aircraft to steer clear.

This building will always be the hangar of my youth. My grandmother, Rose O'Carroll, used to bring us here in her big Cadillac after first giving us a ride around the field.

At Brendan's behest, we walked to the center of the hangar, ducking under the tails of two Gulfstream IV jets. He studied the floor for a moment, then said, "Here it is," as he kneeled down, "Check this out." He motioned for me to examine the spot. I bent down and noticed that this spot was lighter than the rest of the floor due to a patch job to repair a crack. On the patch was written, "Fred, 1968."

I couldn't believe it. Up until now I had kept my emotions in check. But seeing Fred Farbin's signature really lost it for me as the past came flooding back. It was Fred who had fueled Orville Wright's plane. Fred had been hired by my grandfather at the age of 17, and except for a stint in the Merchant Marines, he had never known any other work, spending his whole life at Midway. It was Fred who had secured this hangar when he had heard it was for lease and

Monarch's original hangar on Cicero Avenue was badly in need of repair.

I remembered Fred's infectious laugh and cool sunglasses and his green station wagon. He used to give me jobs as a kid working at the hangar, but an assignment from Fred never seemed like work since it was such a pleasure to be in his company. He would talk to me for hours about the old days and the changes he had witnessed in aviation throughout his life.

I reached down and touched his name in the cement, and held my fingers there for a long moment. "Let's go," I said.

Rose O'Carroll, the author's grand-mother, drives in front of Monarch Air Service's hangar on the west ramp of Midway Airport, 1970.

From the Lynch family collection.

From the Lynch
family collection.

Fred Farbin (with his
wife Delores) celebrates
40 years working at
Monarch Air Service at
Midway Airport, 1984.

Out on the ramp, we turned our attention to the task at hand. Midnight was just a few minutes away, and we had no champagne. What were we to use to toast our final moments on the field? Then it dawned on me. "Of course," I said. "Coffee!" Most appropriate—it was the caffeine boost that pilots, limo drivers, and passengers looked forward to down through the decades. My memories of the airport are as much of the smell of fresh coffee as of jet fumes.

We walked back into the lounge and poured coffee. Red raised his eyebrows. "Dropped the champagne," I said sheepishly as he laughed.

We all gathered in a circle as Monarch's final moments ticked down. "To the memory of Pierce and Rose O'Carroll," I said, as we raised our cups and drank.

Brendan said, "I think that on our last toast we should pour the coffee on the ground." We agreed.

Then it was midnight. We waved farewell to Red, and Brendan, Katie, and I drove quietly out of the parking lot.

It was the end of an era—one of the oldest family-owned aviation business in the United States was no more.

Monarch Air Service

1932–1997

From the Lynch family collection.

✈   ✈   ✈

THE ATTACKS ON the World Trade Center and the Pentagon on September 11, 2001, have changed the way Americans view air travel and airports, probably for good. An outing to Marshall Field's famed Cloud Room at Midway in 1949 was a pleasant experience for the whole family. No fear or worry and no having to stand in long lines or going through metal detectors. When working summers at Monarch during my high school years, we would drop off our customers on the tarmac inside the field while DC-9s taxied a few feet away. Such service would be unthinkable today. Those beautiful Gulfstream jets I used to freely wander around are now patrolled by security guards.

There is no doubt that one of the casualties of Nine Eleven is our lost innocence about airports and air travel. The old rules have been grounded, and the new rules are still being written. The story of Midway Airport, however, might shed some light on how the flying public can move forward from these unsettling times.

Two weeks after September 11, President George W. Bush traveled to O'Hare International Airport to reassure Americans that it is safe to fly. His trip was a welcome one, but in the story of aviation not the first time a national figure flew to Chicago to boost the confidence of a jittery public wary of commercial aviation.

As told earlier in this book, after a plane crash took the life of Notre Dame football coach Knute Rockne in 1931, Franklin D. Roosevelt, then governor of New York, flew to the Democratic presidential convention in 1932 to accept the nomination of his party. He landed at Chicago Municipal Airport (Midway) and by this dramatic gesture demonstrated that flying was safe. The airlines bounced back.

President Bush spoke to a crowd at O'Hare as thousands of airline employees cheered while he was flanked at the podium by two United and American Airlines jets. Commercial air travel is now bouncing back. As FDR did 70 years earlier, GWB demonstrated that in the skies Americans have nothing to fear but fear itself.

✈

A commercial jet lands on runway 4-R at Midway Airport, late 1990s.

BIBLIOGRAPHY

Bernstein, Arnie. *Hollywood on Lake Michigan: 100 Years of Chicago and the Movies*. Chicago: Lake Claremont Press, 1998.

Casey, John A. *Chicago Aviation and Airports: The First Forty Years, 1926-1966*. City of Chicago, Department of Aviation report, 1966.

Cernan, Eugene and Don Davis. *The Last Man on the Moon*. New York: St. Martin's Press, 1999.

Chanute, Octave. *Progress in Flying Machines*. Long Beach, CA: Lorenz & Herweg, 1977.

Chicago Tribune, Stevenson Swanson, ed. *Chicago Days: 150 Defining Moments in the Life of a Great City*. Chicago: Contemporary Books, 1997.

Dodds, Warren "Baby". *The Baby Dodds Story, as told to Larry Gara*. Los Angeles: Contemporary Press, 1997.

Donald, Herbert Donald. *Lincoln*. New York: Simon & Schuster, 1995.

Hill, Robert M. *A Little Known Story of the Land Called Clearing*. Chicago: Chicago Historical Society, 1983.

Jackson, Donald Dale. *Flying the Mail (Epic of Flight)*. Alexandria, Virginia: Time-Life Books, Inc., 1982.

Kirk, Stephen. *First in Flight: The Wright Brothers in North Carolina*. Winston Salem, NC: John F. Blair Publisher, 1995.

Marson, Peter J. *The Lockheed Constellation Series.* Air Britain Publication, 1982.

Miller, Donald L. *City of the Century: The Epic of Chicago and the Making of America.* New York: Simon & Schuster, 1996.

Stevenson Swanson, ed. *Chicago Days: 150 Defining Moments in the Life of a Great City.* Chicago: Contemporary Books, 1999.

White, Richard. *Remembering Ahanagran: Storytelling in a Family's Past.* New York: Hill and Wang, 1998.

Young, David and Neal Callahan. *Fill the Heavens with Commerce: Chicago Aviation, 1855-1926.* Chicago: Chicago Review Press, 1981.

INDEX

- Numbers in italics refer to photographs.

- Specific planes can be found alphabetically under *aircraft*.

About the Author

✈ **Christopher Lynch** has spent most of his life around Midway Airport, where his family ran Monarch Air Service, a fixed based operator (FBO) that serviced aircraft for over six decades until it was sold in 1997. Lynch has always had a fascination with the airport's history, and his research and collection of Midway photos and memorabilia were the basis of the documentary "Midway Airport: Crossroads of the World," part of WTTW-Channel 11's highly-acclaimed *Chicago Stories* series.

Lynch is a graduate of Lawrence University with a B.A. in History and Religious Studies, and also has a private pilot's license. He works in the Public Affairs Bureau for the City of Chicago, Department of Buildings.

Since the recent birth of their triplets, parenting with his wife Cindy has become his most rewarding challenge. Lynch can be reached on the Web at www.midwayhistory.com.

LAKE CLAREMONT PRESS IS . . .

REGIONAL HISTORY

New! Compared with Terkel and Berkow and recommended by *Chicago* magazine, *Chicago Jewish History*, *The Chicago Jewish News*, and others.

Near West Side Stories: Struggles for Community in Chicago's Maxwell Street Neighborhood
By Carolyn Eastwood

Near West Side Stories is a current and ongoing story of unequal power in Chicago. Four representatives of immigrant and migrant groups that have had a distinct territorial presence in the area—one Jewish, one Italian, one African-American, and one Mexican—reminisce fondly on life in the old neighborhood and tell of their struggles to save it and the 120-year-old Maxwell Street Market that was at its core.
1-893121-09-7, June 2002, trade paperback, 6" x 9", 360 pages, 113 historic and contemporary photographs, $17.95

From the author of *To Sleep with the Angels: The Story of a Fire*.

Great Chicago Fires: Historic Blazes That Shaped a City
By David Cowan

As Chicago changed from agrarian outpost to industrial giant, it would be visited time and again by some of the worst infernos in American history—fires that sparked not only banner headlines but, more importantly, critical upgrades in fire safety laws across the globe. Acclaimed author and veteran firefighter David Cowan tells the story of the other "great" Chicago fires, noting the causes, consequences, and historical context of each. In transporting readers beyond the fireline and into the ruins, Cowan brings readers up close to the heroism, awe, and devastation generated by the fires that shaped Chicago.
1-893121-07-0, August 2001, trade paperback, 10" x 8", 167 pages, 86 historic and contemporary photographs, $19.95

- Winner of an American Regional History Publishing Award: 1st Place—Midwest, 2001.
- Winner of the 2000 Midwest Independent Publishers Association Award: Merit Award (2nd Place) in History.
- Nominated for the Abel Worman Award: Best New Book in Public Works History.

The Chicago River: A Natural and Unnatural History
By Libby Hill

When French explorers Jolliet and Marquette used the Chicago portage on their return trip from the Mississippi River, the Chicago River was but a humble, even sluggish, stream in the right place at the right time. That's the story of the making of Chicago. This is the *other* story—the story of the making and perpetual re-making of a river by everything from geological forces to the interventions of an emerging and mighty city. Author Libby Hill brings together years of original research and the contributions of dozens of experts to tell the Chicago River's epic tale—and

intimate biography—from its conception in prehistoric glaciers to the glorious rejuvenation it's undergoing today, and every exciting episode in between.
1-893121-02-X, August 2000, trade paperback, 6" x 9", 302 pages, 78 historic and contemporary maps and photos, $16.95

Literary Chicago: A Book Lover's Tour of the Windy City
By Greg Holden, with foreword by Harry Mark Petrakis
Chicago has attracted and nurtured writers, editors, publishers, and book lovers for more than a century and continues to be one of the nation's liveliest literary cities. Join Holden as he journeys through the streets, people, ideas, events, and culture of Chicagoland's historic and contemporary literary world. Includes 11 detailed walking/driving tours.
1-893121-01-1, March 2001, trade paperback, 5.5" x 8.5", 332 pages, 83 photos, 11 maps, $15.95

"The Movies Are": Carl Sandburg's Film Reviews and Essays, 1920-1928
Edited and with historical commentary by Arnie Bernstein, with introduction by Roger Ebert
During the 1920s, a time when movies were still considered light entertainment by most newspapers, the *Chicago Daily News* gave Sandburg a unique forum to express his views on the burgeoning film arts. *"The Movies Are"* compiles hundreds of Sandburg's writings on film, including reviews, interviews, and his earliest published essays of Abraham Lincoln—which he wrote for his film column. Take a new look at one of Hollywood's most exciting periods through the critical perspective of one of America's great writers. A passionate film advocate, Sandburg early on grasped and delighted in the many possibilities for the new motion picture medium, be they creative, humanitarian, or technological; intellectual, low-brow, or merely novel. In doing so, he began defining the scope and sophistication of future film criticism.
1-893121-05-4, October 2000, trade paperback, 6" x 9", 397 pages, 72 historic photos and artifacts, $17.95

Winner of an American Regional History Publishing Award: 1st Place—Midwest, 2000.
Hollywood on Lake Michigan: 100 Years of Chicago and the Movies
By Arnie Bernstein, with foreword by *Soul Food* writer/director George Tillman, Jr.
This engaging history and street guide finally gives Chicago and Chicagoans due credit for their prominent role in moviemaking history, from the silent era to the present. With trivia, special articles, historic and contemporary photos, film profiles, anecdotes, and exclusive interviews with dozens of personalities, including Studs Terkel, Roger Ebert, Gene Siskel, Dennis Franz, Harold Ramis, Joe Mantegna, Bill Kurtis, Irma Hall, and Tim Kazurinsky.
0-9642426-2-1, December 1998, trade paperback, 5.5" x 8.5", 364 pages, 80 historic and contemporary photos, $15

The Hoofs and Guns of the Storm: Chicago's Civil War Connections
By Arnie Bernstein, with foreword by Senator Paul Simon
Far from the Mason-Dixon line, Chicago and Chicagoans were involved in the War Between the States in ways now often overlooked. Before visiting Gettysburg, Mississippi, or Virginia, use Bernstein's history and guidebook to appreciate the historical tourism available right outside your door! Includes Lincoln sites.
1-893121-06-2, early 2003, trade paperback, 5.5" x 8.5", historic and contemporary photos, $15.95

Our Best-Seller!

Chicago Haunts: Ghostlore of the Windy City

By Ursula Bielski

From ruthless gangsters to restless mail order kings, from the Fort Dearborn Massacre to the St. Valentine's Day Massacre, the phantom remains of the passionate people and volatile events of Chicago history have made the Second City second to none in the annals of American ghostlore. Bielski captures over 160 years of this haunted history with her unique blend of lively storytelling, in-depth historical research, exclusive interviews, and insights from parapsychology. Called "a masterpiece of the genre," "a must-read," and "an absolutely first-rate-book" by reviewers, *Chicago Haunts* continues to earn the praise of critics and readers alike.

0-9642426-7-2, October 1998, trade paperback, 5.5" x 8.5", 277 pages, 29 photos, $15

More Chicago Haunts: Scenes from Myth and Memory

By Ursula Bielski

Chicago. A town with a past. A people haunted by its history in more ways than one. A "windy city" with tales to tell . . . Bielski is back with more history, more legends, and more hauntings, including the personal scary stories of *Chicago Haunts* readers. Read about the Ovaltine factory haunts, the Monster of 63rd Street's castle of terror, phantom blueberry muffins, Wrigley Field ghosts, Al Capone's yacht, and 45 other glimpses into the haunted myths and memories of Chicagoland.

1-893121-04-6, October 2000, trade paperback, 5.5" x 8.5", 312 pages, 50 photos, $15

Graveyards of Chicago: The People, History, Art, and Lore of Cook County Cemeteries

By Matt Hucke and Ursula Bielski

Like the livelier neighborhoods that surround them, Chicago's cemeteries are often crowded, sometimes weary, ever-sophisticated, and full of secrets. They are home not only to thousands of individuals who fashioned the city's singular culture and character, but also to impressive displays of art and architecture, landscaping and limestone, egoism and ethnic pride, and the constant reminder that although physical life must end for us all, personal note—and notoriety—last forever.

0-9642426-4-8, November 1999, trade paperback, 5.5" x 8.5", 228 pages, 168 photos, $15

Haunted Michigan: Recent Encounters with Active Spirits

By Rev. Gerald S. Hunter

Within these pages you will not find ancient ghost stories or legendary accounts of spooky events of long ago. Instead, Rev. Hunter shares his investigations into modern ghost stories—active hauntings that continue to this day. *Haunted Michigan* uncovers a chilling array of local spirits in its tour of the two peninsulas. Wherever you may dwell, these tales of Michigan's ethereal residents are sure to make you think about the possibility, as Hunter suggests, that we are not always alone within the confines of our happy homes. So wait until the shadows of night have

cast a pall over the serenity of your peaceful abode. Then snuggle into your favorite overstuffed chair, pour yourself a bracing bolt of 80-proof courage, and open your mind to the presence of the paranormal which surrounds us all.
1-893121-10-0, October 2000, trade paperback, 5.5" x 8.5", 207 pages, 20 photos, $12.95

Coming Soon!
More Haunted Michigan: New Encounters with Ghosts of the Great Lakes State
By Rev. Gerald S. Hunter
1-893121-29-1, early 2003, trade paperback, 5.5" x 8.5", photos, $15

GUIDEBOOKS BY LOCALS

New!
A Cook's Guide to Chicago: Where to Find Everything You Need and Lots of Things You Didn't Know You Did
By Marilyn Pocius
Pocius shares the culinary expertise she acquired in chef school and through years of footwork around the city searching for the perfect ingredients and supplies. Each section includes store listings, cooking tips, recipes, and "Top 10 ingredients" lists to give readers a jump start on turning their kitchens into dens of worldly cuisine. Includes an easy-to-use index with over 2,000 ingredients! Recommended by the *Chicago Tribune, Chicago Sun-Times, Chicago Reader, Daily Southtown, Local Palate,* Pioneer Press newspapers, *Chicago Life,* ChicagoCooks.com, FoodLines.com, ethnic-grocery-tours.com, and more!
1-893121-16-X, June 2002, trade paperback, 5.5" x 8.5", 278 pages, $15

Ticket to Everywhere: The Best of *Detours* Travel Column
By Dave Hoekstra, with foreword by Studs Terkel
Chicago Sun-Times columnist Dave Hoekstra has compiled 66 of his best road trip explorations into the offbeat people, places, events, and history of the greater Midwest and Route 66 areas. Whether covering the hair museum in Independence, Missouri; Wisconsin's "Magical Mustard Tour"; the Ohio Tiki bar on the National Register of Historic Places; Detroit's polka-dot house; or Bloomington, Illinois—home to beer nuts, Hoekstra's writings will delight readers and instruct tourists. A literary favorite of daytrippers, adventurers, and armchair travelers alike!
1-893121-11-9, November 2000, trade paperback, 5.5" x 8.5", 227 pages, 70 photos, 9 maps, $15.95

ORDER FORM

Chicago's Midway Airport	_____ @ **$19.95** =	_____
Near West Side Stories	_____ @ $17.95 =	_____
A Cook's Guide to Chgo.	_____ @ $15.00 =	_____
Great Chicago Fires	_____ @ $19.95 =	_____
The Chicago River	_____ @ $16.95 =	_____
Literary Chicago	_____ @ $15.95 =	_____
"The Movies Are"	_____ @ $17.95 =	_____
Hollywood on Lake Michigan	_____ @ $15.00 =	_____
Chicago Haunts	_____ @ $15.00 =	_____
More Chicago Haunts	_____ @ $15.00 =	_____
Haunted Michigan	_____ @ $12.95 =	_____
Graveyards of Chicago	_____ @ $15.00 =	_____
Ticket to Everywhere	_____ @ $15.95 =	_____
_____	_____ @ _____ =	_____
_____	_____ @ _____ =	_____
_____	_____ @ _____ =	_____

Subtotal: _____
Less Discount: _____
New Subtotal: _____
8.75% Sales Tax for Illinois Residents: _____
Shipping: _____
TOTAL: _____

Discounts when you order several titles!
2 books—10% off total, 3-4 books—20% off,
5-9 books—25% off, 10+ books—40% off

—**Low shipping fees**—
$2.50 for the first book and $.50 for each additional book,
with a maximum charge of $6.

Order by mail, phone, fax, or e-mail.
All of our books have a no-hassle,
100% money back guarantee.

*Lake Claremont Press books can be
found at Chicagoland bookstores and
online at Amazon.com, bn.com, and others.*

Name_____

Address_____

City_____**State**_____**Zip**_____

E-mail Address _____

*Please enclose check, money order,
or credit card information.*

Visa/Mastercard #_____**Exp.** _____

Signature_____

4650 N. Rockwell St.
Chicago, IL 60625
773/583-7800
773/583-7877 (fax)
lcp@lakeclaremont.com

LAKE CLAREMONT PRESS

ALSO FROM LAKE CLAREMONT PRESS

Near West Side Stories:
Struggles for Community in
Chicago's Maxwell Street Neighborhood
Carolyn Eastwood

A Cook's Guide to Chicago
Marilyn Pocius

Great Chicago Fires:
Historic Blazes That Shaped a City
David Cowan

The Chicago River:
A Natural and Unnatural History
Libby Hill

Literary Chicago: A Book Lover's
Tour of the Windy City
Greg Holden

"The Movies Are": Carl Sandburg's
Film Reviews and Essays, 1920-1928
ed. by Arnie Bernstein,
introduction by Roger Ebert

Hollywood on Lake Michigan:
100 Years of Chicago and the Movies
Arnie Bernstein

Ticket to Everywhere:
The Best of Detours *Travel Column*
Dave Hoekstra

Graveyards of Chicago:
The People, History, Art, and
Lore of Cook County Cemeteries
Matt Hucke and Ursula Bielski

Chicago Haunts:
Ghostlore of the Windy City
Ursula Bielski

More Chicago Haunts:
Scenes from Myth and Memory
Ursula Bielski

Haunted Michigan:
Recent Encounters with Active Spirits
Rev. Gerald S. Hunter

COMING SOON

More Haunted Michigan: New Encounters
with Ghosts of the Great Lakes State
Rev. Gerald S. Hunter

The Hoofs and Guns of the Storm:
Chicago's Civil War Connections
Arnie Bernstein
with foreword by Senator Paul Simon

A Native's Guide to Northwest Indiana
Mark Skertic

A Native's Guide to Chicago, 4th Edition
Lake Claremont Press
ed. by Sharon Woodhouse

Muldoon: A True Chicago Ghost
Story: Tales of a Haunted Rectory
Rocco A. and Dan Facchini

The Firefighter's Best Friend: Lives and
Legends of Chicago Firehouse Dogs
Trevor and Drew Orsinger

Creepy Chicago
(children's book)
Ursula Bielski

Finding Your Chicago Ancestors
Grace DuMelle

Chicago's Midway Airport
(audiobook)
Christopher Lynch

Chicago Haunts
(Spanish Edition)
Ursula Bielski

Lake Claremont Press books celebrate what's distinctive about Chicago's history, culture, geography, spirit, and lore.
Join us in preserving the past, exploring the present, and ensuring a future sense of place for our corner of the globe.